C0-ATI-143

THE INDEBTEDNESS

OF HANDEL

TO

OTHER COMPOSERS

The Indebtedness of Handel to Works by other Composers

By Sedley Taylor

With a New Foreword by
Paul Henry Lang

JOHNSON REPRINT CORPORATION

New York • London

1971

Reprinted by permission of
the Cambridge University Press

First Published
in 1906

Copyright © 1971 by Johnson Reprint Corporation
All Rights Reserved

ML
410
. H13
T2
1971
Library of Congress Catalog Card Number: 78-153959

Johnson Reprint Corporation
111 Fifth Avenue
New York, N.Y. 10003, U.S.A.

Johnson Reprint Company Ltd.
24/28 Oval Road,
London, NW1 7DD, England

Printed in the U.S.A.

ALMA COLLEGE
MONTEITH LIBRARY
ALMA, MICHIGAN

FOREWORD

Every listener to music has, on occasion, been struck by the similarity of one piece to another. At times this similarity is no more than a vague suggestion in his own mind of certain characteristics common to both, but on other occasions he is arrested by whole sections of a composition which not only remind him of other music, but in fact are quotations. Borrowing musical material has been looked upon by musicians for many centuries as a legitimate artistic procedure, indeed, as a first principle. The notion of plagiarism is a fairly recent one; the name for this moral crime was not used until long after the period when musical borrowing had its greatest flourishing, in the Middle Ages and the Renaissance. However, despite the moralists and the lawyers, the practice of musicians has not changed but has continued even into our own day, as can be seen in the works of Bartók, Ives, Stravinsky, and many others. Only, as was not the case during the Renaissance, composers must carefully limit their borrowings to music in the public domain. Yet this interesting interbreeding of ideas, and this is what the borrowing of musical materials really amounts to, created in the minds of nineteenth-century scholars a severe moral dilemma.

The moral issue was raised early in the nineteenth century, when righteous scholars were still dreading a repetition of the professional embarrassment caused by their acceptance of Macpherson's gentle poetic fraud, *Ossian,* and when the rising romantic spirit placed considerable emphasis on originality. In the *Quarterly Musical Magazine and Review* (London, 1822), an author signing himself F.W.H., stated the prevailing attitudes with remarkable directness.

[*vii*]

FOREWORD

As in the moral world the legislation has enacted that a particular species of theft shall be denominated felony, where it is perpetrated under circumstances of atrocity and to a great extent, and punished with the utmost vigour, while the same crime called petty larceny, when of a less injurious nature, where the property stolen is of small value, it is to be followed by a milder punishment; so I conceive the plagiarisms I am about to notice to be called *musical felonies* when *whole* passages, subjects of fugues, and other equally important parts of a composition are pilfered by men whom perhaps, from their previous *good character,* we may be inclined to recommend to mercy; yet, as a warning to others, they must certainly be brought up to the *Harmonic Old Bailey,* where they are to receive the reward for their *crimes* by the verdict of a jury of *critics.* The petty larcenies are those stolen passages which, from their shortness or want of interest, or being clothed in varied harmony are concealed by their adaptor.

Thomas Busby, organist, lexicographer, and critic, tried to defend Handel, against whom the above article was directed, on the ground that he improved the material borrowed. "It has been said of him as of Cicero, that whatever he touched he turned to gold; but it might with more correctness be affirmed that his judgment rejected what was not originally good, and that the gold he borrowed he refined." To this F.W.H. indignantly answered with: "This is the first time I ever heard of a theft being deemed less culpable by the improvement which the robber has afterwards made in the article stolen."

What the romantic moralists did not realize—or did not want to realize—was that in earlier times the mere act of borrowing another musician's piece was a great compliment to the man and his music. This would seem to be particularly true in the case of a model finding repeated use, whether at the hands of many composers or of the same individual. When one musician uses a composition repeatedly, then it is obvious that to him this piece, this model, represents more than just another possibility for polyphonic treatment; it is a model he regards with the greatest of respect and admiration. Johannes Tinctoris, the great fifteenth-century theoretician, usually a sober writer, waxes poetical when he speaks of Ockeghem, Busnois, Caron and Faugues. "As Virgil took Homer for his model in that divine work, the *Aeneid,* so I have used these composers as models for my modest works, and especially in the arrangement of the concords I have plainly imitated their admirable style of composing.'' Gioseffo Zarlino and Pietro Cerone, the acknowledged musical legislators of the Renaissance and the early Baroque, write in the same vein. Indeed, a cursory reading of Cerone's instructions concerning the composition of a Mass gives the impression that the technique of reworking borrowed material is the only method of composition. We should be mindful of the fact that despite this veneration and respect, the model compositions were not considered definitive and unsurpassable. Finally, there is the eternal principle of artistic freedom within self-imposed limitations. Throughout the history of music the composer reveled in the solution of problems, he welcomed and gloried in difficulties to be surmounted. For a long time he valued the original melodic idea less than its elaboration, for even an untutored mind can invent a melody, but only the highly trained master craftsman can take a given melody or melodies and from these devise other harmonious configurations in sound, putting the borrowed elements to work to arrive at a new artistic creation.

The practice of borrowing shows a perceptible pattern of growth. The oldest forms of it in Western music used the borrowed material intact. Later, there was developed the idea of adding new material to the already existing music, and finally that of modifying the borrowings themselves. This we can see from the progression from literal use of a *cantus firmus* to the more complex techniques of paraphase and parody. The simplest approach is of course the borrowing of an entire melody or portion thereof as a *cantus firmus* upon which a composition could be built. The technique of developing the given melody was gradually extended, until in the fourteenth and fifteenth centuries we encounter the elaborately organized isorhythmic structures. The composers also began to ornament the borrowed melody, not infrequently to the point where little resemblance to the original remained. Another favorite device was the subjection of the *cantus firmus* to various canonic elaborations, and still later the *cantus firmus* began to migrate from voice to voice. The most advanced and developed use of the *cantus firmus* technique is a free working out of the borrowed melody in all voices, known as the paraphrase. *The cantus firmus* was an underlying constructive element which lent its own organization to the other voices; a paraphrase, on the other hand, involves the transformation of a melody by means of ornamentation, rhythmic alteration, or other devices for varying the original melodic design; it was these variations of one melody that furnished the substance for all voices in their future activity throughout the piece. Since these melodies used in the paraphrase technique could come from any source, sacred or secular, there remained but one step to the appropriation of a whole composition, all its melodies, all its voices, its harmonic and formal scheme, as the material out of which to construct another composition. This is the so-called parody. (Parody is a somewhat unfortunate musicological term which has no pejorative connotation. It refers to the use of a motet or chanson in vastly elaborated form as the basis for a new composition. The new work is usually named after the borrowed model. Thus, Palestrina's Mass, *Hodie natus est,* is a parody of his motet of the same name.) Thus the composer selects a model and then he quarries his own musical ideas out of the depths of his model. The most important thing in parody composition is the interjection of original and freely invented material into the body of the model. This new material must always follow and dovetail with the preceding and succeeding statements of the model; it must match in mood and style, and yet it must indubitably be the music of the borrower. This was the most elaborate form of borrowing known to musical history. The original may be altered by redistribution, reduction or increase of voices, by insertion of new material by the parodist, by rhythmic alteration, or by inexact quotation resembling the paraphrase.

In the Baroque era the parody technique was less often employed, because the possibilities of altering the guise of a model written for several voices within a chordal framework are considerably less than in the case of those written within a polyphonic-imitative structure. But now theme and variation and a renewed *cantus firmus* and paraphrase technique based on the Lutherna chorale came to the fore; so the principle of composing upon borrowed melodies was still very much alive. The use of stock basses and similar patterns as the subject of variations was widespread in both vocal and instrumental music, and the subjects of canzona, ricercar, and fugue were freely borrowed. Nor was the parody technique proper really forgotten; both Bach and Handel employed what was essentially a parody technique, if less elaborate than that of their Renaissance forebears.

Bach's adaptations of sonatas from Reinken's *Hortus Musicus,* and his many borrowings from Legrenzi, Albinoni, Corelli, Vivaldi, and others are as numerous as Handel's, and so are his parodies of his own works. In fact, he borrowed and reworked compositions to such an extent that the chronology of his works can hardly be established with accuracy. He reworked instrumental numbers into vocal compositions and vice versa, converted secular into sacred cantatas, and so forth. Friedrich Blume raises the question that many of us must have asked time and again. "It is difficult to understand the sense and purpose of these reworkings; in many instances it would have been much simpler to compose a new piece than to completely refurbish old ones." The reasons that induced Bach to do so, I think, are the same that actuated Handel. Something in the composer's unconscious flashes a memory that suits the mood, the affective requirements of the moment; it generates a creative spark, and since the age placed little value on absolute newness, the composer reworked a good and usable idea. But the romantics were not familiar with the historical precedents, nor did they realize that Handel's borrowings were not a painful discovery of posterity but were well known to his contemporaries as well as to the great eighteenth-century historians, Burney and Hawkins, who mentioned them as a matter of course. Unfortunately, the nineteenth century judged things altogether from the point of view of the reigning moral precepts.

Friedrich Chrysander, Handel's first modern biographer, and the editor of the great Händelgesellschaft edition of the composer's

FOREWORD

collected works, decided in 1888 to challenge this uninformed and unfair view, an act which in those days required considerable scholarly courage. Then in 1906 Sedley Taylor dedicated the first scholarly publication to the question, the work reprinted here. It not only illuminates the whole matter but affords a fascinating study of the working of an exceptional musical mind, for upon what may be called Handel's "transplant technique" an entire course in musical composition could be based.

Paul Henry Lang

CAMBRIDGE UNIVERSITY PRESS WAREHOUSE,

C. F. CLAY, Manager.

London : FETTER LANE, E.C.

Glasgow: 50, WELLINGTON STREET.

ALSO

London: AUGENER AND CO.

Leipzig: F. A. BROCKHAUS.

New York: G. P. PUTNAM'S SONS.

Bombay and Calcutta: MACMILLAN AND CO., Ltd.

[All Rights reserved.]

THE INDEBTEDNESS

OF

HANDEL

TO WORKS BY OTHER COMPOSERS

A PRESENTATION OF EVIDENCE

BY

SEDLEY TAYLOR M.A.
FORMERLY FELLOW OF TRINITY COLLEGE, CAMBRIDGE

Cambridge
at the University Press
1906

PREFACE.

IN the following pages I attempt to place before my readers sufficient materials for forming an independent judgment on Handel's indebtedness to the works of a number of composers who were his predecessors or contemporaries.

The task of singling out the compositions on which he appears to have drawn most largely, and the labour of publishing them, have been already performed, principally by the late Dr Friedrich Chrysander, ably followed by Dr Max Seiffert. But something, I thought, still remained to be done in the presentation of this pioneer-work, before its results could become effectively accessible to musicians in general.

The published editions of "Handel-sources" were, indeed, prefaced by full references to the places in his works where he had used specified passages from them, but the process of comparison still necessitated the acquisition of half-a-dozen such volumes and of a dozen works by Handel, followed by the hunting-up and confronting of the corresponding passages, not unfrequently complicated by the need of transposition.

Convinced that nothing would persuade the British musical public to take all this trouble, I determined to present in a single volume a study of the whole subject, based on a selection from the above-mentioned materials, doing my best by suitable collocation of musical extracts, aided, wherever requisite, by transposition, to render the process of comparison as easy. as possible.

PREFACE

After an Introduction which sketches the history of opinion as to Handel's originality, five chapters are occupied in proving that he borrowed as freely from the compositions of other masters as he worked up into new shapes earlier productions of his own.

In chapters VI and VII a full presentation is made of the processes by which older materials were transformed—sometimes really *transfigured*—into large portions of that choral masterpiece, *Israel in Egypt*. The contents of these chapters will, I venture to hope, prove of permanent value to students of composition, as they afford a close view of Handel obtaining some of his mightiest effects by methods of the most unexpected and wonderful character.

The concluding chapter contains a discussion of the question whether Handel was morally justified in dealing as he did with works by other composers.

My various personal obligations are acknowledged in the sequel at the points where they are severally incurred, but I wish here to thank the Syndics of the Fitzwilliam Museum in this University, by whose kindness I am enabled to publish extracts from the Handel autographs preserved in their custody, which have a decisive bearing on the subject treated in this volume.

My cordial thanks are due to my friend Dr Charles Wood, who read the work in manuscript and afforded me valuable assistance during its passage through the press.

SEDLEY TAYLOR.

Trinity College,
Cambridge,
July, 1906.

TABLE OF CONTENTS.

TABLE OF CONTENTS

CHAPTER VII.

CHAPTER VIII.

INTRODUCTION.

HANDEL'S mode of turning to account the works of other composers is
characterised by a writer in the *Encyclopædia Britannica* in the following
uncompromising terms:

"The system of wholesale plagiarism carried on by him is perhaps unprecedented in the history of music. He pilfered not only single melodies but
frequently entire movements from the works of other masters, with few or no
alterations and without a word of acknowledgment."[1]

With this it is instructive to compare an equally sweeping, but diametrically
opposite, assertion on the same topic made by Sir John Hawkins about
seventeen years after Handel's death:

"And here it may not be impertinent to observe, what every person con-
versant with his works will be inclined to believe, viz. that his style was
original and self-formed: and were evidence of the fact wanting, it is capable
of proof by his own testimony, for in a conversation with a very intelligent
person now living, on the course of his studies, Mr Handel declared that,
after he became master of the rudiments of his art, he forbore to study
the works of others, and ever made it a rule to follow the suggestions of
his own fancy."[2]

I adduce this statement solely in order to show that during, and for some
years after, Handel's life-time no whisper of his being a plagiarist had reached
a man so well situated for hearing it as was Sir John Hawkins. That Handel,
after reaching maturity, forbore to study the works of other composers, admits,
as will be seen later, of such decisive refutation that I cannot believe him
to have asserted it, and prefer to attribute to Hawkins the acceptance of
incorrect information from his anonymous source.

[1] Article 'Handel,' written by the late Mr F. Hueffer, 1880.
[2] History of Music, vol. v. p. 412.

INTRODUCTION

Handel's earliest biographer, Mainwaring, also lays stress on his originality as a composer, describing "that grandeur of conception which predominates in his choruses" as "coming purely from Nature," and saying that "in his fugues and overtures he is quite original" and that "the style of them is peculiar to himself and no way like that of any Master before him."[1]

It is interesting to hear the distinguished composer of the beautiful glee "By Celia's Arbour," William Horsley, taking, half-a-century later, the same ground with even greater emphasis:

"If ever there existed a musician who could lay just claim to originality, that man was Handel. He drew all his stores from Nature and from the force of his own genius and was indebted to no one either for his style or his thoughts. He could not bend his talents to think after anybody else; conscious of the strength of his own powers, he disdained imitation, and trusted confidently to them alone. His music therefore is, properly speaking, his own. . . . ."[2]

This judgment fairly represents, I think, the practically axiomatic belief in Handel's originality entertained by the bulk of English musicians until quite recent times.

A very different opinion had meantime been gradually forming itself, the progress of which shall next be traced.

Burney, in the preface to his "Account of the Musical Performances in Westminster Abbey and the Pantheon in commemoration of Handel,"[3] which took place in 1784, says something which may imply that, a quarter of a century after Handel's death, a tendency to question his absolute originality had begun to make itself heard. Writing in the following year (1785), Burney remarks:

"I know it has been said that Handel was not the original and immediate inventor of several species of Music for which his name has been celebrated, but with respect to originality it is a term to which proper limits should be set before it is applied to the productions of any artist." He goes on to explain that "The scale, harmony and cadence of Music being settled, it is impossible for any composer to invent a *genus* of composition that is *wholly and rigorously new*, any more than for a poet to form a *language, idiom and phraseology* for himself."[4] Whether the objections which Burney had in view here were of such a kind as could be fairly met by these somewhat platitudinous considerations we are left uninformed. Some twenty years later,

---

[1] "Memoirs," London, 1760, pp. 192 and 202.
[2] This passage is taken from an article in the *Quarterly Musical Review* for 1818, p. 282. The article is unsigned, but in my copy of the volume containing it, which belonged to my grandfather, Richard Mackenzie Bacon, who was then Editor of that periodical, it is headed in manuscript "W. Horsley, Esq."
[3] London, 1785.   [4] Preface, p. 39.

however, the charge of plagiarism was formulated against Handel with the utmost directness by no less a person than Samuel Wesley, one of the best organ-players of his time, author of that admirable 8–part motet, "*In exitu Israel*," and father of the still more celebrated composer, Samuel Sebastian Wesley. In a letter to his friend Jacob, dated Oct. 19, 1808, he wrote as follows :

"Salomon has said truly and shrewdly enough, that the English know very little of the Works of the German Masters, Handel excepted, who (as he observes) came over hither when there was a great dearth of good Musick, and here he remained (these are his words) establishing a Reputation wholly constituted *upon the spoils of the Continent*. This would nettle the Handelians desperately, however it is the strict truth, for we all know how he has pilfered from all manner of Authors whence he could filch anything like a thought worth embodying."[1]

There can be no doubt that, if Handel had committed such depredations on Continental compositions, the celebrated German violinist Salomon (1745–1815) was exceptionally qualified, by varied experience on the Continent and long residence in England, to detect and expose them. But, whatever was the source whence Wesley derived his information, he evidently claims for himself, his correspondent and their associates, a direct knowledge of the "pilferings" and "filchings" here attributed to Handel.

In 1831 the names of twenty-nine composers, whose works he asserted to have been laid under contribution by Handel, were published by Dr William Crotch, then Professor of Music in the University of Oxford :

"Handel quoted or copied the works of Josquin de Prez, Palestrina, Turini, Carissimi, Calvisius, Uria[2] (*sic*), Corelli, Alessandro and Domenico Scarlatti, Sebastian Bach, Purcell, Locke, Caldara, Colonna, Clari, Cesti, Kerl, Habermann, Muffat, Kuhnau, Telemann, Graun, Mondeville, Porta, Pergolesi, Vinci, Astorga, Bononcini, Hasse, etc."[3]

Further, in his published adaptations of Handel's works for the organ or pianoforte, and in some manuscript notes of his preserved in the Library of the British Museum, Crotch proceeded to allege details by giving lists of passages in Handel's works which he asserted to have been borrowed from, or modelled on, specified compositions by other masters. To these I shall have occasion to recur when we come directly to compare portions of Handel's works with the passages from compositions by other masters from which they are asserted to have been

---

[1] Letters of Samuel Wesley to Mr Jacob edited by his daughter. London : Partridge & Co. 1875. p. 9.

[2] Should be Urio.

[3] "Substance of several courses of Lectures on Music." London : Longman and others. 1831. Note on p. 122.

derived. To do this in Crotch's time was possible only to erudite and exceptionally well situated musicians like himself, the works from which Handel was alleged to have borrowed being then for the most part unpublished and practically inaccessible.

This state of things lasted for more than another half-century until Dr Friedrich Chrysander, well known as the learned biographer of Handel and as the Editor of the great German edition of his works, brought out, as "Supplements" to that edition, between the years 1888 and 1892, a series of five volumes containing compositions to which, in his opinion, Handel was principally indebted.

These compositions, arranged in the order of their publication, are : 1. Erba's *Magnificat*. 2. Urio's *Te Deum*. 3. A Serenata by Stradella. 4. A collection of duets by Clari. 5. Gottlieb Muffat's harpsichord pieces entitled "*Componimenti Musicali*." To these must now be added an edition of Keiser's opera 'Octavia' which was left in a complete state by Dr Chrysander at his death, in 1901, and has since been published under the care of his literary executor, Dr Max Seiffert, as No. 6 of the Handel "Supplements." Each of these volumes, with the exception of No. 2, contains a preface enumerating the passages in Handel's works where the composition in hand has been drawn upon. An edition of four oratorios by Carissimi, from whom Handel also borrowed, had been published by Chrysander at an earlier date, independently of the Handel Society and without any reference to the use which Handel had made of them.

In 1903 Dr Seiffert effected an important advance in an article[1] on Franz Johann Habermann containing large extracts from masses by that composer, together with precise indications of the places where, and the extent to which, Handel had used them. Dr Seiffert is careful to explain that it was Chrysander's intention, if his life were prolonged, to prepare an edition of Habermann's masses to form the next number in his series of Handel "Supplements." Lastly, in 1905, Dr Seiffert published[2] the collected works of Friedrich Wilhelm Zachow[3], organist at Halle, and the only teacher in executive music and composition that Handel ever had.

These works show very few traces of creative power, which perhaps explains why Handel seems to have borrowed next to nothing from them. But they constitute evidence that Zachow had an easy control over the forms of composition with which a choirmaster in an important North German church at the end of the seventeenth century had to deal, and that he was accordingly well fitted to lay a durable foundation for his great pupil's future superstructure.

In enquiring what is actually proved by the valuable published matter cursorily described above, we shall be materially assisted by evidence contained in the collection of Handel autograph manuscripts preserved in the Fitzwilliam Museum of the University of Cambridge.

---

[1] Published in the *Kirchenmusikalisches Jahrbuch*, Regensburg : Pustel, 1903, pp. 81—94.

[2] In the *Denkmäler Deutscher Tonkunst*.

[3] Or, as his name has hitherto been spelt, Zachau.

INTRODUCTION

A number of its pages contain movements—some complete, some incomplete, some consisting of mere fragmentary scraps a few bars long—which used to be regarded as compositions, or sketches for compositions, of Handel's own, but have now been in numerous cases identified as extracts made by him from works by other composers, not a few of which have analogues in his published writings. Where, in such instances, a question of priority arises, evidence that one of the parties knew, and copied from, the work of the other is obviously of great weight. We shall in the sequel come across several instances in which decisive evidence of this kind is supplied by the Fitzwilliam autographs.

We will now proceed to a detailed comparison between portions of Handel's works, and passages in those of other composers from which they are asserted to have been—with greatly varying degrees of alteration, curtailment and addition—directly taken. The number and extent of the instances where this is alleged are so very considerable, that to apply such a comparison to anything like all of them would entail a process of huge length and portentous wearisomeness. Selected cases are, therefore, all that can be dealt with here, and these will be grouped under the names of the several composers from whose works the appropriations are alleged to have been made.

When the printing of this volume was already in its final stage, an accident recalled my attention to certain arguments published, in a letter to the *Musical Times*[1], by Mr P. Robinson, of Manchester, supporting the view that Handel may have composed not only the *Magnificat* attributed by Chrysander to Erba, but also the *Te Deum* and the *Serenata* ascribed by him to Urio and Stradella respectively. I read that letter at the time of its appearance, but afterwards, to my regret, allowed its contents, which ought to have been noticed in the sequel, to escape my memory while I was engaged on the present work. All, therefore, that I can now do is to refer my readers to Mr Robinson's letter, leaving to further research the task of investigating the issues which he has raised in it.

[1] December, 1905.

CHAPTER I.

COMPARISON OF PASSAGES FROM WORKS BY HANDEL WITH EXTRACTS FROM COMPOSITIONS BY GOTTLIEB MUFFAT, AND WITH MANUSCRIPT COPIES MADE THENCE BY HANDEL.

GOTTLIEB MUFFAT (1690-1770), of Vienna, was one of the best composers of his time for the harpsichord. His chief work, entitled "*Componimenti Musicali per il Cembalo,*" is a collection of overtures, fugues, fantasias etc., and of movements in dance-forms, minuets, rigaudons, sarabandes, gigues and the like. The resemblances between eighteen of these and passages in Handel's works which have been specified by Chrysander are of such a kind as to make it manifest either that Handel copied from Muffat or Muffat from Handel. We have, therefore, to decide between these alternatives. Unfortunately the date at which Muffat's '*Componimenti*' were published is so uncertain that it cannot be relied on as an element of comparison. The late Herr C. F. Pohl, in an article on Muffat in Grove's Dictionary of Music,[1] stated that the work in question was published at Vienna in 1727, and he made a memorandum to that effect in a copy of the '*Componimenti*' in the Library of the *Gesellschaft der Musikfreunde* at Vienna, of which he was then Librarian.[2] On the other hand Chrysander in his edition of the '*Componimenti*' reproduces the original title-page which states that the work was printed at Augsburg, but bears no date. In the German[3] preface Muffat describes his good fortune in having met with his famous "engraver and publisher" ("*Kupferstecher und Verleger*") who had produced ("*verfertiget*") the work to his entire satisfaction. According to this evidence, therefore, the '*Componimenti*' were printed and published at Augsburg, not at Vienna as stated by Pohl. The fact that the date is wanting on the original title-page affords, of course, no proof that Pohl did not possess some independent evidence capable of establishing it. For us, however, the date which he assigns, 1727, rests on his assertion only. Chrysander, on conjectural grounds, considered the work to have been published "about the year 1735,"[4] but, as this view depends on the assumption that "Handel had the '*Componimenti*' in his hand in 1739 or perhaps a year earlier,"[5] no weight can, without circular reasoning, be assigned to it at the present stage of our enquiry.

---

[1] First edition.

[2] This fact was kindly communicated to me by Dr. Mandyczewski, the present librarian of the *Gesellschaft*, who added that he was unable to ascertain on what ground Pohl, who was generally very accurate in statement, based his fixation of the date and place of publication of Muffat's work.

[3] The preface appears also in Italian, but in the corresponding passage mentions the *printer* ("*Impressore*") only.   [4] Preface to his edition of Muffat's '*Componimenti*.'   [5] *Ibidem*.

B

So far, then, the external evidence is inconclusive, but an appeal to that supplied by the Fitzwilliam Handel autographs will prove much more fruitful. These contain certain disjointed musical scraps, of from 3 to 5 bars each, which so experienced a Handelian scholar as Dr. A. H. Mann has not been able to recognize as appearing anywhere in Handel's published works, but which he and I between us have identified as agreeing in minute detail with passages in Muffat's '*Componimenti.*' This renders it very improbable that Muffat took these passages from any Handelian source, as he certainly had no access to Handel's private note-books; and therefore establishes a strong probability that Handel copied them from Muffat's published volume. A detailed comparison between the forms in which these passages are presented in the note-books and in the '*Componimenti*' will, I think, make it clear that Handel was here the copyist. To this comparison we now proceed.

Ex. 1.

The occurrence in Handel's version of only one tie (bar 3) as against six in Muffat (bars 3 and 4) is an indication that Handel is here copying, not composing. The absence of a flat before E (H. bar 4, Bass, first note) shows that a tie should have been inserted as in Muffat. In the same bar the second B ought to have a flat before it as in Muffat. The absence of a flat before E (H. bar 2, Treble) and of a 'natural' before the second F (H. bar 3, Bass) tells the same tale.

Ex. 2.

At the beginning of Handel's autograph here he has first written in the Treble clef and then crossed it out and replaced it by the Soprano clef, which was doubtless that used in Muffat's original edition. The upper stave in the autograph opens thus

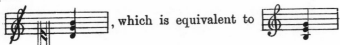, which is equivalent to

and not consistent with the Bass. I conjecture that Handel made the change
of clef *after he had written in the opening chord,* and forgot to alter it
correspondingly when he replaced the Treble by the Soprano clef in which
therefore it reads as the chord of E minor instead of as that of G major.

Immediately after Handel's "etc." comes a further fragment corresponding to
a passage in Part II. of the same Allemande by Muffat, the Treble clef being this
time used by Handel.

Ex. 3.

Here the difference of barring makes Handel's version much the better of the two. We cannot suppose that Muffat had it before him and deliberately worsened its vigorous accentuation, and therefore must here see Handel copying from Muffat and improving on him while doing so.

Ex. 4.

Handel's version here looks on the face of it anything but like a bit of original composition. It begins with a chord in four parts followed by another in three, both provided with Thorough-Bass figuring from which we learn nothing but what the chords themselves tell us. Next come five notes of Treble and Bass only, with incomplete figuring, then six unfigured chords in five parts and one in four. Bars 3 and 4 show wrong notes, A and A♭ appearing in one and the same chord in Bar 3, and B and B♭ in bar 4.

It is hardly possible to imagine Handel putting his own ideas on paper in this fashion, but quite easy to suppose him jotting down these notes and scanty figures if his object was to produce, not a copy of what Muffat had written, but a rough memorandum sufficient to recover its salient features if he should subsequently have occasion to make use of them. So far it has, I think, been established that Handel copied out, or made memoranda of, passages from Muffat's 'Componimenti.'

I place next an example showing Handel at work elaborating a fine accompanied recitative out of apparently unpromising materials taken from the same quarry.

Ex. 5.

Accompanied Recitative from the *Ode for St. Cecilia's Day*.

Na - ture un - der-neath a heap of jar - ring A - toms

lay And could not heave her head.

An argument already used above, is equally applicable to this case. Had Muffat seen Handel's unaccompanied recitative he could not by any possibility have reduced it to the dead level of his *Adagio*. Therefore it must have been developed by Handel on the skeleton supplied by Muffat. It is immediately followed in the *Ode for St. Cecilia's Day* by short unaccompanied recitatives, alternating with two instrumental interludes identical, save for slight alterations, with passages from a 'Fantaisie' by Muffat, as is shown in the next example:

Ex. 6.

Ex. 6 (continued.)

The superiority of Handel's part-writing in Ex. 6, bar 2, and of his distribution of parts in the second part of that example suffice, as in previous instances, to show that he must here, too, be regarded as copying from, and improving on, Muffat.

The comparisons made above suffice, I think, to establish the fact that Handel borrowed from Muffat.   I add three more, however, before passing away from this composer, on account of their possessing special points of interest; the first and second as being, with the exception of judicious excisions, slight modifications of key and filling in of harmonies, entire movements simply 'lifted off' Muffat; the third as showing where Handel got the stirring subject of the allegro in his well-known overture to *Samson*.

Ex. 7.

In Muffat's original the key-signature is *three* flats. I have omitted his very numerous 'graces' here and in the next example.

Ex. 8.

Ex. 9.

Handel.
Allegro
in
Overture
to
Samson.

Muffat.
Fantaisie.
p. 122.

CHAPTER II.

FRANZ JOHANN HABERMANN (1706-1783) was a composer of Bohemian birth to whom, as Dr. Max Seiffert has shown in a most interesting article,[1] Handel is under considerable obligations for material taken from five[2] masses published by him in 1747 and incorporated by Handel in his *Jephtha* which was composed in 1751. The question of priority is thus decisively settled by external evidence, confirmed, as will immediately be seen, by the Fitzwilliam autographs.

The extracts from Habermann's Masses, which will now be compared with the corresponding passages in Handel's works, are all taken from Dr. Seiffert's article.

Ex. 10.

Handel. *Jephtha.*

Violins. 1st & 2nd

Bass.

Habermann. *Mass I.*

Violins.

Organ.

[1] *Kirchenmusikalisches Jahrbuch :* Regensburg, 1903.

[2] *Ib.* p. 83. A sixth mass followed in Habermann's volume, but in Dr Seiffert's opinion it was not drawn upon by Handel.

Han.

No more to   Ammon's god and   king,   fierce

Hab.

Ky - ri - e   e   -   lei   -   - son,   e -

C

* - - - - * Compare the passages thus marked.

The whole of the extract from Habermann given in Ex. 10 appears, copied out in full in Handel's handwriting, but without words or composer's name, in the Fitzwilliam autographs.[1] This fact supplies, of course, independent evidence, were such wanted, of Handel's indebtedness to Habermann.

The comparisons made in the next six Examples will speak for themselves.

Ex. 11.

HANDEL. Symphony to the song "His mighty arm with sudden blow." *(Jephtha.)*

Strings.

HABERMANN. *Mass I.* Introduction to *"Rex cœlestis."*

Violins.

Transposed
a Major
Third
down.

Handel.
F. W. Auto-
graphs.
(H. 13. p. 75.)
Transposed
a Major
Third
down.

Ex. 12.

Ex. 13.

Handel.
Jephtha.

Theme su-blime of end-less praise, of end-less

Theme su-blime of end-less

Alla breve. O - san-na

Habermann.
Mass I.
Transposed
a Major
Third down.

O - san-na   in   ex-cel - - - sis, in - - - ex-   Seiffert's
Extract
ends.

Handel. F. W.
Autographs.
(13. p. 90.)
Compressed
from open
score and
transposed
a Major
Third down.

Alla breve. "Theme sublime of endless Praise." *(MS.)*

etc.

Ex. 14.

Alto.

Handel.
Jephtha.

Orchestral
Bass.

Che - - mosh   no   more will we a-dore with tim-brell'd

an - thems to Je-ho-vah   due, with tim-brell'd an - - - thems
Che - - - mosh   no

Habermann. *Mass I.*

Cum san-cto   spi - ri - tu   in
Cum   san - - cto

Handel. F. W. Autographs.
(13. p. 88.)
Compressed from open score.

Ex. 15.

Instrumental Introduction to the Song "Hide thou thy hated beams." *(Jephtha.)*

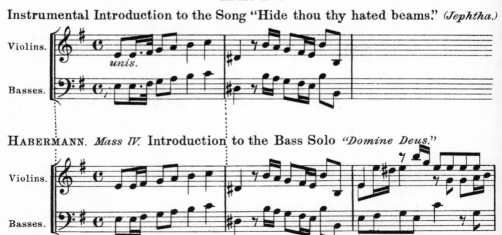

HABERMANN. *Mass IV.* Introduction to the Bass Solo *"Domine Deus."*

By striking out Habermann's feeble and inconsequent third and fourth bars, and similar matter in his seventh and eighth bars, Handel has greatly improved this little prelude.

Ex. 16.

Symphony to the Song "Pour forth no more unheeded prayers." *(Jephtha.)*

HABERMANN. *Mass I.* Symphony to Chorus *"Kyrie eleison."*

Violins.

Transposed
a Major Third down.
Organ.

This song, which in *Jephtha* occupies 115 bars, is mainly built on these materials, and the accompaniment is throughout made from Habermann's.

CHAPTER III.

GIOVANNI CARLO MARIA CLARI (1669—about 1740) was a distinguished maestro di capella who wrote a large amount of sacred and secular music. Among the latter were a number of vocal duets, passages in which find more or less close homologies in Handel's *Theodora*. These passages are contained in six of the duets produced, according to Chrysander, "about 1720" and published by him, with the exception of one duet, from a "contemporary copy" in his own possession. The excepted duet he inserted from a Paris edition published a century later, in 1823. The Fitzwilliam Museum possesses manuscript copies of thirty-seven trios and duets by Clari, including the six which concern us here: each of these is marked either '1740' or '1741'—dates which Mr. Fuller-Maitland thinks probably refer to the first edition of the duets.[1] This would give a date some twenty years later than that assigned by Chrysander, assuming—which I do not feel sure of—that by 'produced' he meant 'published,' and not merely 'composed.' In any case it may be safely inferred from the dates affixed to the Fitzwilliam copies that these six duets were in existence by the year 1741. This clears the question of priority, as Handel's *Theodora* was not performed until 1749.

The method employed by Handel in dealing with the materials supplied by Clari was quite uniform. It consisted in taking thence short themes fit, or capable by slight alterations of being rendered fit, for contrapuntal treatment, and then working them up by all sorts of fugal, canonic and imitative devices applied with astonishing force and freedom, into elaborate polyphonic movements of the well-known "Handelian" type. In this manner several entire choruses and a long orchestral movement are, with more or less infusion of other matter, developed out of passages of two or three bars each taken from Clari's unpretentious but charming little compositions. As, later in the present work, we shall see the same method applied with supreme skill and stupendous results in one of the grandest of all Handel's oratorios, I shall content myself with but a single illustration of its employment on Clari's duets, viz. the construction of the chorus "While Grace and Truth" in *Theodora*.

---

[1] 'Catalogue of the Music in the Fitzwilliam Museum.' p. 152. The Fitzwilliam copies are provided with *figured* basses, which does not appear to have been the case with those edited by Chrysander.

Ex. 17.

This phrase is constructed by assigning to one voice what Clari divides between two voices.

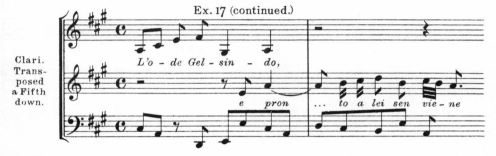

This is followed by

We next come on this theme in Canon:

The use of the scale-passage in Handel's Bass here appears to have been suggested by the following bars of Clari:

This chorus of Handel, consisting of 60 bars, is entirely worked up out of the above materials from Clari's duet.

CHAPTER IV.

KARL HEINRICH GRAUN (1701-1759), a six years younger contemporary of Handel, was a German composer of the greatest distinction and public repute, who held posts of *Capellmeister* at the Courts of Brunswick and Berlin, and whose masterpiece, the oratorio *Der Tod Jesu*, occupies in Germany "in some measure the position which is held by the *Messiah* in England."[1] That Handel should have transferred almost note for note to his own scores the bulk of two choruses of considerable length taken from a work by one of his most eminent contemporaries seems antecedently incredible. That he did this in the case of a work of Graun's has nevertheless been incontrovertibly proved by Professor Prout[2] who was enabled to discover the fact by a concatenation of coincidences so extraordinary that my readers will, I feel sure, wish to be made acquainted with it. I proceed therefore to give an abridged account of his article, sometimes using his own words.

The late Rev. J. R. Lunn, a Yorkshire clergyman and excellent musician, formerly Fellow of St. John's College, Cambridge, was asked by a neighbouring Musical Society to recommend them a Handel chorus for performance. He chose the chorus "Ere to dust is changed that beauty" from *The Triumph of Time and Truth* (1757), but, while he was examining it, the idea struck him that it resembled a movement which he remembered having copied at Cambridge from Latrobe's Collection of Sacred Music.[3] Mr. Lunn hunted up his old manuscript which contained (1) the chorus "Ere to dust" substantially complete but with different words, (2) three bars of adagio, (3) another chorus (in F minor) also with English words, which, shortened by nine bars, he found, set to Italian words, in Handel's *Il Trionfo del Tempo*, an earlier version of the same work, brought out in 1737, which likewise contained the chorus "Ere to dust" set to Italian words. Both these choruses and the connecting *Adagio* were described by

---

[1] Grove's Dictionary of Music, 1st edition.

[2] In an article published in the *Monthly Musical Record* for May and June, 1894.

[3] "Selection of Sacred Music from the works of some of the most eminent composers of Germany and Italy." By C. I. Latrobe. Its six volumes appeared, according to an article in Grove's Dictionary (1st edition), between 1806 and 1825.

Latrobe as taken from an "Oratorio Passionale" composed by Graun. Mr. Lunn, puzzled by this ascription to another of what he had always regarded as the property of Handel, communicated with Professor Prout, who at once took the view that, considering Handel's known habits in such matters, the music was more likely to be Graun's than his, and so Latrobe probably in the right.

Soon after this correspondence with Mr. Lunn, Professor Prout spent a few days at Cambridge with Dr. A. H. Mann, who promptly conducted him to the Library of the Fitzwilliam Museum, to examine the Handel autographs. Dr. Mann took down at random the first volume of the collection, the pages of which Professor Prout began turning over. On pp. 21 and 22 he came upon two scores which had till then been regarded as original drafts for the two choruses mentioned above as having both appeared in the *Trionfo del Tempo*, while but one of them was included in the long subsequent English version of that work. Prout, with the facts to which Mr. Lunn had directed his attention fortunately still fresh in his mind, at once perceived that these scores were not in the form which the Handel choruses in question bear in his published works, but in that of the two movements and intervening short adagio printed as Graun's in Latrobe's collection. This fact, together with a remarkable absence of corrections in these autographs as compared with other original scores of Handel, and with a further piece of evidence to be described in the next paragraph, led Prout to the conclusion that these two choruses were no compositions of Handel, but copies made by him from some, probably unpublished, work by Graun.

The next three pages of the Fitzwilliam autographs contain ten detached movements, or parts of movements, described in the printed catalogue as "at present unidentified." Below, or in the margin of, several of these Handel has written disjointed German words or pairs of words, and this is also the case in the short adagio already mentioned. No one had yet discovered the significance of this curious proceeding, but Professor Prout at once hit on the conjecture that these movements, equally with the two choruses which preceded them in the autographs, were extracts made by Handel from Graun, and that the German words were taken from the text to which Graun's music was set, and jotted down by Handel as clues to enable him to recover with ease the passages in Graun's work from which he had been copying.

Prout soon found himself able to produce decisive confirmation of his theory. He took with him from the Fitzwilliam Museum a German second-hand music-seller's catalogue, as he had noticed a score of Cherubini's in it which he wished to order, and the librarian had handed over the catalogue to him as of no further use to the Museum. On looking through this catalogue he found that it announced for sale an old manuscript score of a ' Passion ' by Graun.

Prout, after making some enquiries which convinced him that this would prove to be the unpublished work from which Handel had borrowed, wrote for and obtained it. On turning over its first page, which was occupied by a choral, he came at once on the two choruses, and the intervening adagio, exactly as they stand in Latrobe. This left but a single link wanting to complete the proof that Graun was their author, viz. evidence of the priority of his ' Passion ' to Handel's *Trionfo*. Such evidence was to hand on Prout's manuscript score which described the work as the ' Brunswick Passion,' from the name of the place where it was produced. Graun is known to have settled in Brunswick in 1725 and to have quitted it in 1735. The latter is, therefore, the latest limit of time for the production of his ' Passion,' whereas Handel's *Trionfo* was not performed till 1737. This accordingly settles the question of priority and with it that of the authorship of the two choruses.

On examining the rest of Graun's score Prout found in it, with one insignificant exception, all the fragmentary movements which follow the two choruses in the Fitzwilliam autographs. Moreover, in every case where Handel had appended German words, as described above, he " found the same words at the same place in Graun's score."

Finally Prout identified about half of these fragments as having been made use of by Handel in *Alexander's Feast*, the *Wedding Anthem*[1] and the operas *Atalanta* and *Giustino*. These works having all been brought out in 1736,[2] Graun remains in a clear priority.

Professor Prout sums up as follows the truly " extraordinary chain of circumstances " which led him to this discovery :

" Had Mr. Lunn selected any other chorus than " Ere to dust," and had he not also, thirty or forty years before, copied the same chorus from Latrobe, he would not have written to me on the subject. Had Dr. Mann happened to take down from the shelves at the Fitzwilliam Library any other one of the fourteen[3] volumes of Handel's manuscripts than the one he took, I should never have seen the extracts from Graun in Handel's writing—and that too at a time when the matter was fresh in my memory, owing to Mr. Lunn's letter, and my having looked at Latrobe only a few days before. Still more remarkable, if possible, was the incident of the catalogue. Had not my eye been caught by the score of Cherubini's, I should not have asked to copy it, and thus received the catalogue. But the most curious thing of all is that this catalogue, which by the merest chance was lying on the table, instead of having been thrown into the waste-paper basket, where I should never have seen it, should contain the very work needed to reveal the truth—a manuscript score, which probably does not come into the market once in twenty years."

Examples 18, 19 and 20 embody three of Prout's five identifications mentioned above.

---

[1] In the case of the *Wedding Anthem* Dr. Mann had already recognised the connexion with one of the Handel fragments.   [2] Grove's Dictionary.   [3] Their number is *fifteen*.

D

Ex. 18.

Instrumental Introduction to the song *"Nacque al bosco"* in *Giustino*.

Introduction to the duet *"Jesu wirst Du zu mir sprechen?"*

Ex. 19.

Part of the Introduction to the song *"Dall' occaso in oriente"* in *Giustino*.

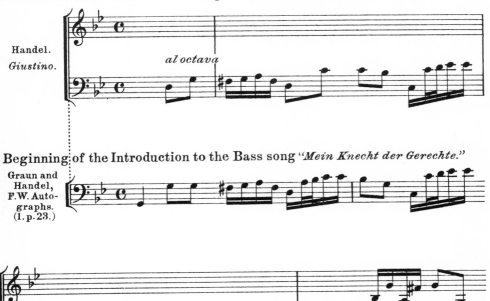

Beginning of the Introduction to the Bass song *"Mein Knecht der Gerechte."*

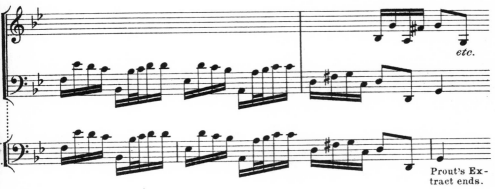

Ex. 20.

Fugue-subject in the chorus *"At last divine Cecilia came"* in *Alexander's Feast*.

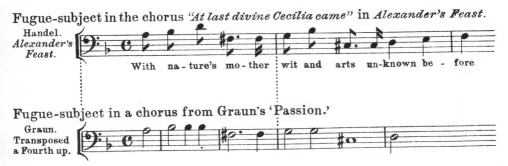

CHAPTER V.

HANDEL'S USE OF EARLIER COMPOSITIONS OF HIS OWN. INSTANCES OF THIS IN THE CASE OF SOME DUETS SET TO SECULAR ITALIAN WORDS AND AFTERWARDS DEVELOPED INTO SEVERAL CHORUSES AND A DUET IN THE *MESSIAH*.

IT has, I think, been adequately shown in the preceding chapters that Handel made free and extensive use of compositions by other masters. But he also treated in precisely the same manner older work of his own, sometimes merely re-setting it, with insignificant modifications, to fresh words, sometimes excising, amplifying or altering it with absolute freedom. We shall subsequently examine instances in *Israel in Egypt* where he did this with magnificent results: here I shall set out a very striking series of transferences and contrapuntal developments to be seen in his working up of some vocal duets, which he had already composed to secular Italian words, into great choruses and a duet in the *Messiah*. All but one of these Italian duets were written only a few months before the composition of that oratorio.[1]

In the following comparisons I shall quote leading subjects from movements in the *Messiah* together with their all but identical originals in the Italian duets. The order followed will be that of the movements in the oratorio: the Italian duets will be quoted from the German Handel Society's edition.

Ex. 21.

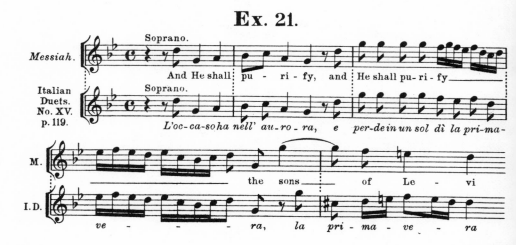

---

[1] Chrysander, Life of Handel, vol. I., p. 371.

The running passage in bar 4 of the duet seems suggested by the word 'primavera' (spring), but is hardly appropriate to the word 'purify' to which it is set in an extended form in the chorus. Handel appears to have felt that something more was wanted than an assemblage of rather mechanical passages and been promptly moved to that stroke of genius the mighty episode:

Ex. 21 (continued.)

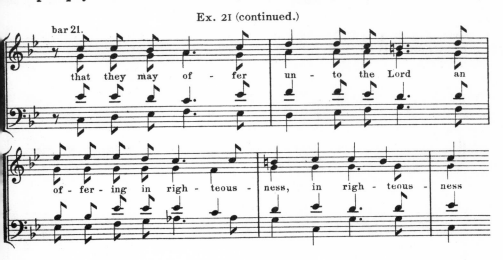

which, repeated in a higher part of the scale and with somewhat modified harmonic treatment, closes this chorus with such impressive grandeur.

Ex. 21 (continued.)

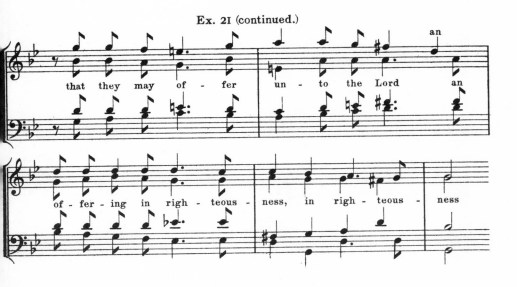

The next two examples show the original destination of subjects which,

contrapuntally treated, make up the bulk of the famous chorus "For unto us a
child is born."

Ex. 22.

Ex. 22 (continued.)

Into this chorus, also, Handel introduced a stroke of genius additional to the material derived from his duet, the great choral shouts:

Ex. 22 (continued.)

The next example has a special interest as clearing up a difficulty which has doubtless puzzled many admirers of Handel as it used to puzzle me. It occurs in the leading subject of the chorus "His yoke is easy and His burthen is light," where the first syllable of the word 'easy' is set to the following almost grotesquely inappropriate passage:

Ex. 23.

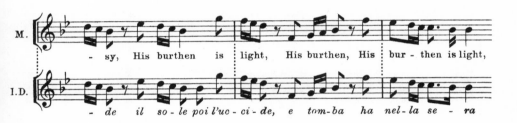

Why Handel should have perpetrated such a monstrosity was to me an insoluble *crux*. A glance, however, at the text to which the passage was originally composed suffices to explain the difficulty: "The flower which laughs at dawn is killed by the sun and finds a grave in the evening." The passage with which we are concerned is set to the word '*ride*' (laughs) and is therefore evidently a piece of word-painting, quite appropriate in its original position, but grievously out of place where it now stands.

The added stroke of genius, for which here too we do not look in vain, ends the chorus with a passage in which beauty and dignity are wondrously mingled.

Ex. 23 (continued.)

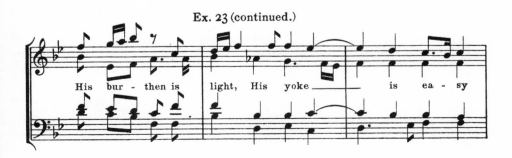

And His bur - - - then is light.

The allegro of the chorus "All we like sheep have gone astray" is wholly built on subjects from a duet the earlier part of which had already been drawn upon for the chorus "For unto us a child is born." They are set out in Ex. 24.

Ex. 24.

Messiah.

Italian Duets. No. XVI. p. 127. Transposed one Tone down.

Bar 3   All we like sheep have gone a - stray

Sò per pro - va   i   vos-tri in-gan - - - ni

Ex. 24. (continued.)

M.   Bar 11   We have tur - - - - - ned

Tenor.   We have tur - ned

H.

I.D.   due ti - ran - - - - - ni

due ti - ran - ni

M.   Bar 15   ev' - ry one to his own way, ev' - ry one to his own way:

Tenor.   ev' - ry one to his own way

H.

I.D.   Soprano I.   due ti - ran - ni, due tì - - - ran - ni sie-te og - nor,

sie-te og - nor

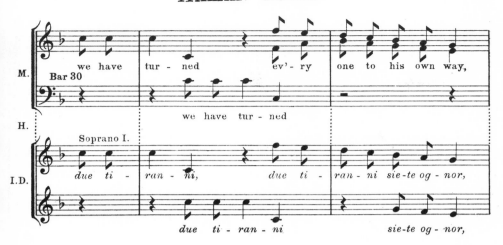

The Italian text is a defiance of "blind love and cruel beauty" whose tyranny and deceits are roundly denounced from personal experience. The music set to this breathes, when transferred to the chorus, a certain heaven-defying reckless-ness which a less dramatically-minded composer than Handel would hardly have read into the English words. Arrived, however, at the point where he had thoroughly worked out the material before him, we see this wonderful man girding himself for a final stroke and making the very audacity with which he had treated his text supply him with the means of producing a magnificent effect of contrast. Abruptly changing the time to *adagio* and passing into minor harmony, he bids the voices enter in solemn canonic sequence, and his chorus ends with a combination of grandeur and depth of feeling such as is at the command of consummate genius only.

Ex. 24 (continued.)

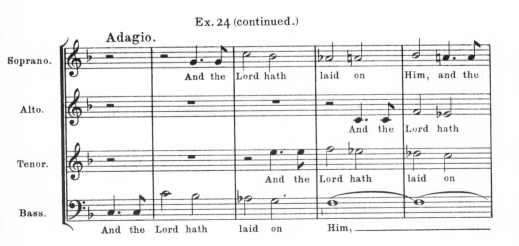

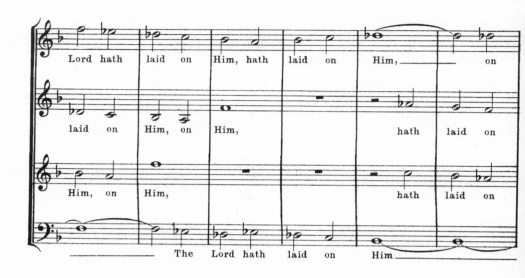

Beside the Italian duets quoted from above there are others written by Handel much earlier, according to Dr. Chrysander as far back as 1712-1720.[1] The music of one of these, set to an exhortation to abandon love, is used in the *Messiah* in the duet "O death where is thy sting?" and also occurs as a subject in the succeeding chorus "But thanks be to God:"

[1] *Life of Handel*, vol. I., p. 367.

Ex. 25.

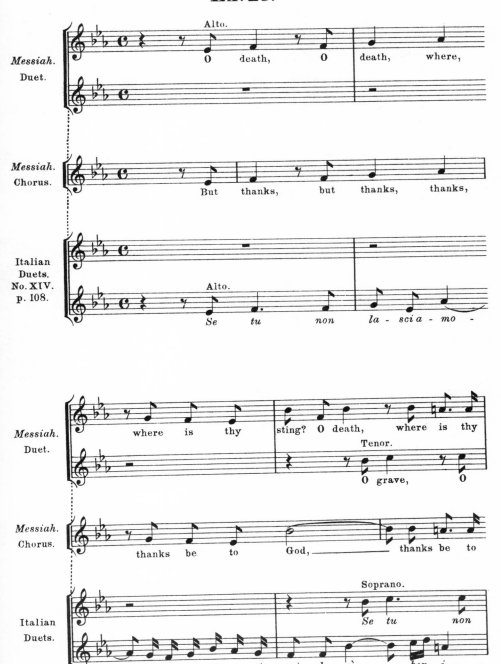

Messiah. Duet. — Alto. O death, O death, where,

Messiah. Chorus. — But thanks, but thanks, thanks,

Italian Duets. No. XIV. p. 108. — Alto. *Se tu non la - sci a - mo -*

Messiah. Duet. — where is thy sting? O death, where is thy | Tenor. O grave, O

Messiah. Chorus. — thanks be to God, _____ thanks be to

Italian Duets. — Soprano. *Se tu non* | *- re, mio cor, ti pen - ti - rai, lo sò ____ ben i - -*

Some instances, rendered especially interesting by their occurrence in the *Messiah*, have now been produced of the freedom with which Handel utilized compositions of his own which had already done duty in a different sphere.[1] They are the only ones which have been detected in that masterpiece, where, so far as research has at present gone, not a single instance has been found of the introduction of music not composed by Handel himself. One would fain hope that this immunity is inherent in that sublime work by the deliberate will of the composer, whose religious emotions are known, from his own statement, to have been deeply stirred while he was engaged on it.

---

[1] A few general remarks on such transferences will be found on pp. 164, 165.

CHAPTER VI.

CHARACTER OF RESULTS ATTAINED BY HANDEL WHEN MAKING USE OF PRE-EXISTING MATERIALS. *ISRAEL IN EGYPT* AFFORDS UNIQUE OPPORTUNITIES FOR STUDYING THESE RESULTS. DETAILED COMPARISON OF PART I. OF THAT ORATORIO WITH PORTIONS OF A SERENATA BY STRADELLA, AN ORGAN-PIECE BY KERL AND FOUR EARLIER COMPOSITIONS OF HANDEL'S OWN.

THE fact of Handel's borrowings from other composers' works, and rearrangements of his own, may now, I think, be regarded as established, and we have to consider what is a still more interesting and instructive subject, viz. how he dealt with his sources, what kinds of effect he succeeded in working them up into, and what is the result of comparisons instituted between the merits of his completed work and those of the compositions utilized in their construction.

It happens that Handel's choral masterpiece *Israel in Egypt* affords an unique opportunity of seeing his mode of procedure carried out on a great scale, and with results of stupendous grandeur which dwarf into insignificance the, often very meritorious, compositions used in producing them. I propose, therefore, in order to bring all this out, to make a full examination of that truly astonishing work in reference to the various sources which are now known to have been drawn upon during its construction.

No antecedent sources are known to exist for the first three numbers, viz. the recitative "Now there arose," the double chorus "And the children of Israel sighed" and the recitative "Then sent He Moses." No. 4, the chorus "They loathed to drink of the river, He turned their waters into blood" is formed out of an organ-fugue, No. 5 of a set of six which Handel wrote in 1720,[1] but did not publish until 1735, three years before he composed *Israel in Egypt*. The fugue, which stands in the key of A minor, consists of 74 bars. Handel cut out 32 of these and transposed the rest, extensively remodelled, into the key of G minor. In the following Example I give the entire chorus together with all the corresponding matter of the organ-fugue which, for convenience of comparison, I have transposed into the key of the chorus.

---

[1] Chrysander : Life of Handel, vol. III. p. 201.

Ex. 26.

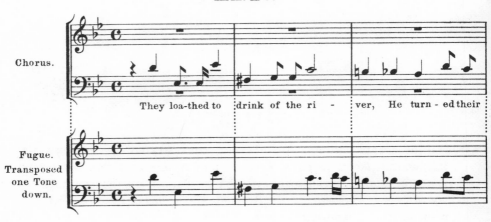

Chorus.

They loa-thed to drink of the ri - ver, He turn-ed their

Fugue.
Transposed
one Tone
down.

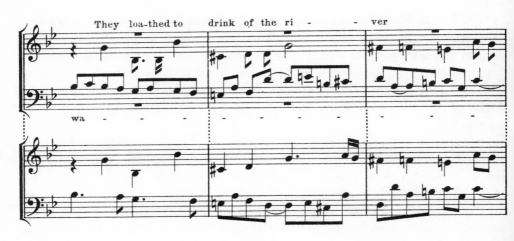

They loa-thed to drink of the ri - - ver

wa - - - - - - - - -

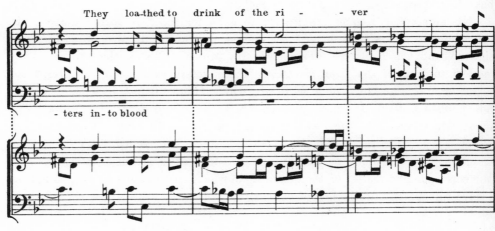

They loa-thed to drink of the ri - - ver

- ters in-to blood

Ex. 26 (continued.)

They loa - thed to drink of the ri - - -

They loa - thed to drink of the ri - - ver

ver

They loa-thed to drink of the ri - -

E

Ex. 26 (continued.)

Ex. 26 (continued.)

They loa-thed to

9 bars
not used.

Ex 26 (continued.)

drink   of   the   ri - - ver,   He   turn - ed their

wa - ters   in - to blood;

they loa - thed to drink   of the ri - ver.

In turning this old organ-fugue into a chorus Handel has evidently effected great improvements in the disposition of his parts, especially in bars 22, 23, 33-36, 38-40. But a power of a much higher order is recognizable in the imagination which could discern in a not exactly inspiring organ-piece the makings of a choral picture so gruesomely descriptive as that which Handel has succeeded in producing. It suffices to play over on the pianoforte first the passages quoted from the organ-fugue and then the chorus, giving effect in the latter to the entries of the subject on "They loathed" and the descending chromatic scale-notes, in order to realize how astonishing this power is.

The Air "Their land brought forth frogs" has not been shown to be derived from any antecedent source.

The ensuing double chorus, (No. 6), " He spake the word," is taken, as far as the choral parts are concerned, with few, but very effective, improvements, from a secular serenata composed by Alessandro Stradella. This will, therefore, be the proper place to tell the little that is known about that composer, from whom, as will presently be seen, Handel took a good deal of material.

ALESSANDRO STRADELLA was a celebrated Italian composer in the seventeenth century and became the central figure of a romantic story which was afterwards put upon the stage as an opera.[1] Subsequent researches having reduced the historical value of this story to zero, we learn from Herr Eitner[2] that the course of Stradella's life is "wrapped in complete darkness." The dates of his birth and death are unknown and nothing of him but a large number of compositions appears to remain.

A score of one of these, entitled "Il Barcheggio," bears evidence that it was composed for a wedding-festivity which took place in 1681. This date is written on two pages of the score, as is also a statement that Il Barcheggio was Stradella's last "sinfonia" or "composizione."[3] No question of priority, therefore, can arise between a work by Handel and one by Stradella, whose last composition is thus fixed at a date four years earlier than Handel's birth.

Dr. Chrysander published, in 1888, as No. 3 of his "Supplements,"[4] an edition of the serenata by Stradella which concerns us here, together with indications of where Handel had used it. The movement on which the chorus "He spake the word " is built up is an orchestral interlude for two separate groups of instruments, one scored for two violins and a bass, the other for a quartet of strings with doubled parts. These two groups alternate with each other throughout the movement in phrases varying from half-a-bar to two bars in length. This arrangement may well have suggested to Handel the idea of turning the movement into a double

---

[1] Set to music both by Flotow and by Niedermeyer in the same year, 1837, (Art. in Grove's Dictionary.)   [2] Musikalisches Quellen-Lexicon, article ' Stradella.'

[3] Grove's Dictionary. 1st ed. vol. III. p. 723 note 4.   [4] See ante p. xi.

chorus, which is what he did by adding a fourth part to Stradella's smaller group, revising his counterpoint with occasional masterly touches and composing descriptive passages of orchestral accompaniment. Handel's chorus and the movement from Stradella's Serenata—the latter taken from Dr. Chrysander's edition—are given in full in the following example:

Ex. 27.

And there came all man-ner of flies,

He spake the word,

Handel.

Stradella
p. 33.

He   spake the word,

And there came all man-ner of   flies,   and there came

12

He spake the word,

lice,   and there came all man-ner of flies and lice in

and there came all man-ner of flies and lice in

all their quar - ters,

all their quar - ters,   He   spake the word,   and there

17

He spake the word,   and there came all manner of flies,

He spake the word, and there

22

23

all their quar - ters, He spake the word,

came all man-ner of flies,   He spake the word,

H.

25

He spake the word,   He spake the

S.

And there came all man-ner of flies and lice in all their quar -

word,

ters,

H.

28   29

and there came all man-ner of   flies and lice in   all their quar -

S.

He spake,   and the lo - custs came with-out

30   31

- ters,   He   spake,

num-ber and de-vour'd the fruits of the ground,

H.

and the lo-custs came with-out

S.

Handel opens his chorus with seven bars based on Stradella's material, but in five of these the sopranos and altos alone take part. Thus a *sforzando* effect is produced when, after bar 8, where continuous borrowing from Stradella begins, mixed-voices harmony is for the first time heard.

In bar 12 Handel obtains increased vigour by his added D in the first choir and by lowering Stradella's semi-quavers an octave.

In bar 17 the two choruses overlap on the 3rd beat with a greatly enhanced effect, which is heard again in bars 22, 23 and 25.

In bars 22 and 23 there is a fine free movement in the two soprano parts where Stradella has none.

In bars 28 and 29 the counterpoint is immensely improved.

In the last beat of bar 30 and the first of bar 31 a wonderful impression of finality is conveyed by the Octave rise of the basses and the Fifth drop of the sopranos on "He spake," where nothing of the kind exists in Stradella. Handel has reinforced these improvements by an accompaniment of florid violin-passages in demi-semiquavers, which pervades the whole chorus, to suggest the buzzing of the flies, and in bars 31-34 by a moving bass in semi-quavers, to illustrate the heavier calamity of the locusts coming "without number" to "devour the fruits of the ground." Chrysander remarks that "the originality of the chorus rests upon this accompaniment."[1] Only if the narrowest and most literal meaning be assigned to "originality" can I admit this. In a higher sense true originality appears to me to be required in order to discern in Stradella's simple, and a trifle jog-trot, piece of chamber-music the potentiality of being developed into a chorus which should present with almost terrifying energy the issuing of the supreme behest and its dire fulfilment. As was well said half-a-century ago:

"The imitation of the buzzing of insects in the accompaniment to Handel's chorus in *Israel in Egypt* "He spake the word and there came all manner of flies" were merely an ingenious trifle, but for the superlative grandeur of the choral passages which tell of the Almighty fiat."[2]

The orchestral introduction to the next, the famous "Hailstone," chorus, (No. 7), probably the greatest popular favourite of the entire oratorio, is made up of eleven bars taken from the opening of the 'Sinfonia' to Stradella's *Serenata*, and four from that to a bass song in the same work, the former standing in the key of D, the latter in that of A. Handel's contribution to his own prelude consists at most in three original bars as against fifteen taken from Stradella.

---

[1] Life of Handel vol. III. p. 66.
[2] Townsend : "Visit of Handel to Dublin:" Dublin 1852 p. 92.

Ex. 28.

ISRAEL IN EGYPT

Stradella p. 50.
(Transposed
a Minor Third up.)

The fine flowing passage set to the words " ran along upon the ground " is
written on a bass in Stradella's song, the second bar of which had already appeared
in the symphony to it, and been incorporated in Handel's sixteenth bar:

Ex. 28. (continued.)

Finally an energetic phrase is taken from the same song, and its force greatly
intensified by the repetition of its first bar and the extension of its descending
scale.

Ex. 28. (continued.)

Of the chorus proper, apart from the opening symphony (which is repeated at
the close, cut down to half its length and with no original matter introduced) nearly
one-half is mere rearrangement, or contrapuntal development, of the phrases from
Stradella which have been set out in Ex. 28.

It cannot be denied that these supply the most interesting material to be found
in the chorus, but there remain as Handel's property the vigorous alternating
entries of the two choirs and the wonderful choral shouts of " fire " first with simple
accompaniment and at last with a magnificent moving bass. But, when all has
been said, we are no nearer to understanding how it was that Handel could detect
the possibilities which lay hid in these, to ordinary observers rather uninteresting
passages, and work them up with other matter of his own into a colossal sound-

picture, vivid, sublime, instinct with a terrible energy and perfectly homogeneous from one end to the other. While we must, I think, rank the power of doing this less highly than that of producing an entirely original composition of equal merit, the name of genius can hardly be refused to it when it attains such results as are embodied in the "Hailstone chorus."

Passing over No. 8, the chorus "He sent a thick darkness," which appears to be original, we come to No. 9, the chorus "He smote all the first-born of Egypt." The subjects of it are taken from another of the set of organ-fugues mentioned above,[1] but, as the treatment of them diverges widely after their first entry, it will suffice to compare the opening eight bars of the two compositions, as is done in the next Example:

Ex. 29.

The next chorus (No. 10), "But as for His people," consists, of 168 bars of which 117 appear to be Handel's property, while 51 are evidently made out of a phrase in a soprano song in Stradella's Serenata which Handel has transferred bodily, with its canonic accompaniment shortened by one bar, as shown in the next Example:—

Ex. 30.

Handel first makes his Altos sing this phrase in the key of G and then his Sopranos in that of C (as in the Example): next the Tenors sing it in the same key, the Altos chiming in at the end with an ingeniously constructed little imitative tag,

Ex. 30. (continued.)

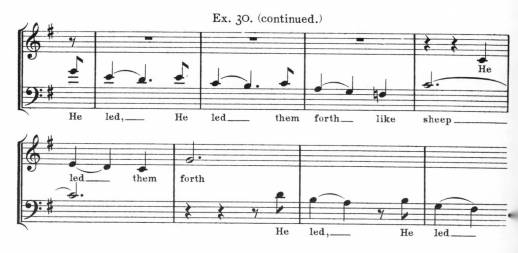

after which the Basses sing the phrase and the Tenors the tag. Finally the Sopranos sing the phrase again in the key of D, the other voices taking over Stradella's figure of accompaniment, shortened as before, and the Sopranos emphasizing the close by an octave drop simultaneously with the entry of the Basses :

Ex. 30. (continued.)

In this manner, if we count in two bars of orchestral continuation, Stradella's phrase of eight bars is elongated into thirty-nine. Later on in the chorus his bit of canonic imitation appears first for the Basses and Tenors and then for the Altos and Sopranos:

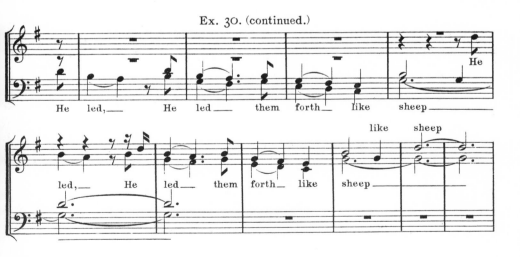

Ex. 30. (continued.)

which, with two more bars of orchestral finish, complete the tale of fifty-one bars which Handel has contrived to spin out of Stradella's phrase of less than nine bars. But for all that, the effect produced is unflaggingly fresh and completely congruous with the words sung.

The chorus which comes next in order, (No. 11), "Egypt was glad when they departed" presents an instance of appropriation which is extreme even for Handel. A celebrated German organist JOHANN CASPAR KERL (1628-1693) published at Munich in 1686, one year after Handel's birth, a work entitled *Modulatio Organica super Magnificat.* A *canzona* contained in that work reappears, with hardly any alterations beyond what were required to adapt an organ-piece for performance by voices, as the chorus now before us. The following Example in which I have printed Kerl's *canzona* as it appears in an undated edition published at Amsterdam[1] will make this surprising fact quite manifest.

Ex. 31.

Chorus "Egypt was glad when they departed."

[1] Kindly placed at my disposal by Dr. A. H. Mann.

"For the fear of them fell upon them."

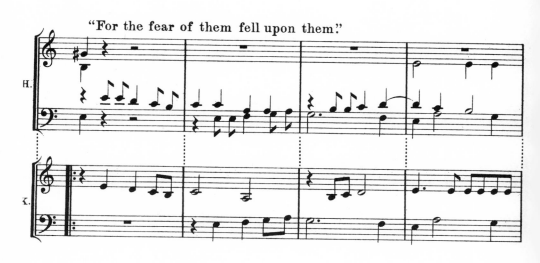

G

As Kerl published his *canzona* in 1686, when Handel was only one year old, his priority is beyond dispute. Curiously enough Sir John Hawkins, in his 'History of Music,' which appeared in 1776, published an inaccurate version of this *canzona* "as a specimen of Kerl's style of composition for the organ," [1] evidently in entire ignorance of the use to which Handel had turned it, 38 years earlier, in *Israel in Egypt.*

Fortunately nothing prevents our regarding the next chorus (No. 12), "He rebuked the Red Sea," as anything but what it has always been taken for—a tremendous stroke of original genius. The remark attributed, I think, to Beethoven, that when Handel chose, he could "strike like a thunderbolt," thoroughly applies to these mighty eight bars. Nor does the inspiration take any lower level in that superb oceanic commingling of sublimity and loveliness, the chorus (No. 13) "He led them through the deep," though for its original form Handel went back more than thirty years to a work which he had composed in Rome in 1707,[2] a setting of Psalm CX. in Latin (*Dixit Dominus*) for a five-part chorus, orchestra and organ. A double fugue in this work to the words "*Tu es sacerdos in æternum secundum ordinem Melchisedech*" contains the germ from which the chorus now under consideration was developed.

In the Psalm,[3] the movement opens as follows, the Basses singing the first subject while the upper voices take the much shorter and quicker second subject in canonic imitation and development:

Ex. 32.

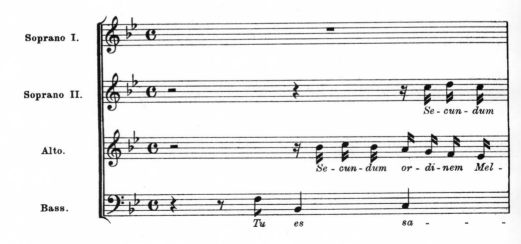

[1] Vol. V. p. 96.   [2] Chrysander : Life of Handel, vol. I. p. 162.
[3] Which I quote from the German Handel Society's edition, vol. 38, p. 79.

In *Israel in Egypt* the double chorus opens by the Basses giving out the first subject accompanied, in unison, by the instrumental basses only, but instead of singing the whole octave-scale as in the Psalm, they plunge down a Seventh upon the word 'deep' with a wonderfully fine effect:

Ex. 32. (continued.)

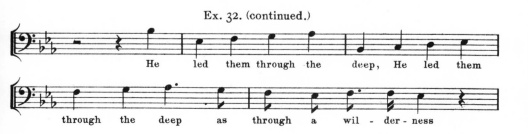

In the last Soprano entry of this subject the plunge is deferred, with increased effect until close upon the end of the subject:

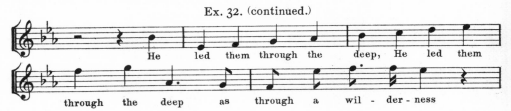

Ex. 32. (continued.)

He led them through the deep, He led them

through the deep as through a wil - der - ness

The second subject, modified in various ways, is constantly at work throughout, first in the orchestra only and then both there and in the voices. Thus the opening of the Psalm-movement gives a rough scheme which is adhered to in the double chorus, but with a richness and exuberant variety of effects which make the earlier composition, fine as it undoubtedly is, pale into comparative insignificance.

The companion picture describing the destruction of Israel's pursuers is drawn with tremendous force in the following chorus (No. 14) "But the waters overwhelmed their enemies." The original idea for this too was taken by Handel from one of his earlier works, the Chandos anthem "The Lord is my light" composed between the years 1717 and 1720[1] while he was music-director to the Duke of Chandos. It appears there in the form of the orchestral prelude[2] to a soprano song set to the kindred words "It is the Lord that ruleth the sea:"

Ex. 33.

Chorus.

But the wa-ters o - ver-

Orchestra.

Anthem.
(Prelude.)

[1] Chrysander: Life of Handel, vol I. p. 458.
[2] Which I quote from the German Handel Society's edition, vol. 35, p. 198 sq.

etc.

The short, but extraordinarily impressive, double chorus (No. 15), "And Israel saw that great work," contains such palpable discharges of creative energy that it may, I hope, be set down to Handel's sole initiative. It is followed by the chorus (No. 16), "And believed the Lord," consisting of 63 bars, 46 of which, *i.e.* nearly three-quarters of the whole chorus, are, with but small modification, taken from, or built up on, a soprano song accompanied by two violins and a bass in Stradella's *Serenata*. Example 34 sets out the first 17 bars of the chorus with the corresponding passages in the song:

Ex. 34.

After four bars of continuation on these materials Handel produces (bars 22-31) the following burst of inspiration :

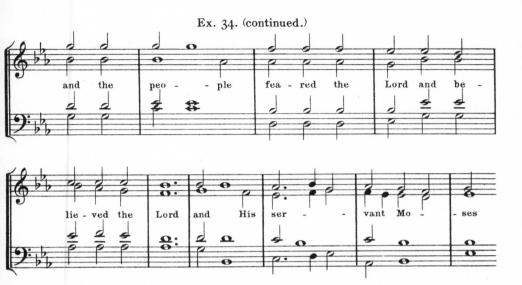

Ex. 34. (continued.)

The rest of the chorus reverts to the Stradella material except in bars 45-52 where a descending scale-passage of four notes receives the following fine treatment in canon :

Ex. 34. (continued.)

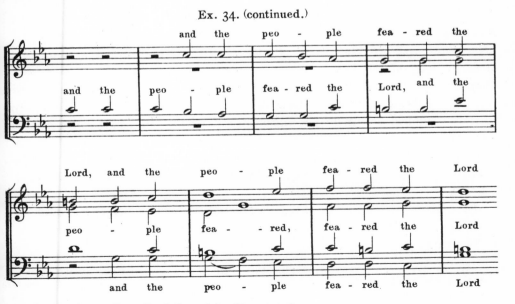

With this chorus Part I. of *Israel in Egypt* ends.

CHAPTER VII.

WE have seen the use that Handel made of a serenata by Stradella in the first Part of *Israel in Egypt*. In the second Part he made a still more extensive, indeed well nigh exhaustive, use of a Latin *Magnificat* set for double chorus, orchestra and organ, the authorship of which presents a problem of much interest. Only two manuscript copies of it are known to exist, one in Handel's own handwriting, but without indication of authorship, which is preserved in the Royal Library at Buckingham Palace, the other in a different handwriting and inscribed "Magnificat Del Rᵈ Sigʳ Erba,"[1] which is preserved in the Library of the Royal College of Music. After what we have seen of Handel's copying of choruses by Graun in the Fitzwilliam autographs, the mere existence of this Magnificat in his handwriting cannot be accepted as proof that he composed it; indeed, in the opinion of Dr. Chrysander, Handel's manuscript presents clear internal evidence of not being an original work but a copy, and probably made from separate 'parts,' not from a score. The Royal College manuscript, on the other hand, supplies a piece of positive evidence by assigning the composition of the Magnificat to a priest (Rᵈ Sigʳ) named Erba. It has, however, been maintained by two supporters of the Handelian authorship that the words "Magnificat Del Rᵈ Sigʳ Erba" meant only that the manuscript score now in the Library of the Royal College was once the *property of*—not had been *composed by*—the person named in the superscription. "I suppose," wrote, in 1857, Mr. (afterwards Professor Sir) G. A. Macfarren, "this superscription to signify that the copy had belonged to a Signor Erba."[2] "The obvious meaning of this inscription," asserted, in 1883, Mr. W. S. Rockstro, "is that the volume in which it is written had once belonged to a Priest named Erba. Had the *Magnificat* been composed by Signor Erba, the word used would have been 'dal, not 'del.'"[3]

In order to test the truth of the idiomatic rule thus confidently laid down by Rockstro, I examined the titles of many old Italian manuscript scores in the Fitzwilliam Library.

---

[1] Mr. Barclay Squire informs me that the third word of this inscription may be read either as 'Sigr' or as 'Sgr' and that the handwriting has too little character to be used as decisive evidence to show whether the copyist was Italian or English.

[2] Preface to an analysis of *Israel in Egypt* written for the Sacred Harmonic Society in 1857.

[3] Rockstro: Life of Handel: Macmillan and Co., 1883, p. 222.

The following are a few of these titles, which, it will be observed, are exactly parallel to the " Magnificat Del R^d Sig^r Erba " of the Royal College score :

F. W. Library Classmarks	*Title-pages.*
30 F 7 No. 4	Messa . . . Del Sig^r: Alesandro Scarlatti
23 F 4 p. 212	Messa . . . del Sig^r: D. Leonardo Leo
24 F 9 p. 1	Oratorio . . Del Sig Alesandro Stradella
22 F 25 p. 1	Duetti per Cammera Del Sig^r: Abbate Stefani
24 F 4 p. 33b	Cantate Domino del Sig^r Silvestro Durante
30 F 7 p. 37	Dixit . . . del Mol^o: R^o: P: M: G: B^a: **Martini**
22 F 12 [cover]	Fetonte opera orig[ina]le del Sig^r Paradies
22 F 6 p. 1	Dixit . . . . Del Sig^r: D: Nicola Jommelli celebre Maestro

These examples suffice to refute the assertion that *del*, thus used, denotes mere ownership. *That*, indeed, used to be indicated in a different way. Thus in the preface to Bach's organ works, vol. III. p. XIV. of the Leipzig edition, a manuscript is mentioned entitled " Sonata per il cembalo solo del Sigr J. S. Bach, poss. J. G. Müthel" and on the following page another entitled: "Fuga clamat[1] in B♮ di Johann Seb Bach Poss. Joh Peter Kellner." The persons to whose names 'poss.' [*i.e.* 'possessore' or 'posseditore'] is prefixed are as evidently the *owners* of these scores as Bach is the *composer* of the sonata and of the fugue.

The general result of my inspection of a large number of manuscript title-pages was that, for the purpose of designating authorship, 'del' was in much the most common use, that 'di' was not unfrequently employed and that 'da' and 'dal' were but rarely met with.

We are now, I think, entitled to conclude that the entry on the Royal College manuscript was meant to assert that the R^d Sig^r Erba *composed* the Magnificat written on its pages.

It remains to enquire who Erba was, and on this point we are again indebted to the researches of Dr. Chrysander. In his 'Life of Handel'[2] he has shown that a composer of much distinction, Don Dionigi Erba, was in the year 1694 writing opera for Milan, and may well have been the author of our 'Magnificat.' The prefix 'Don' indicating that he was a priest, agrees with the 'R^d Sig^r' of the Royal College score, and the laying out of the work for a double chorus is consistent with its having been composed for the 'duomo' at Milan where "opportunities were afforded, principally by means of two large organs placed facing each other, for keeping the old polychoric church music longer in use than in the rest of Italy."[3] On these grounds Chrysander conjecturally assigned the composition of the Magnificat to Dionigi Erba. Its style, he wrote, "is not in the most remote

---

[1] I do not know what ' clamat ' means in this connexion.   [2] Vol. I. p. 173.
[3] *Ib.* p. 175. My friend Mr. E. J. Dent tells me that he has frequently seen organs thus placed in churches elsewhere in Italy.

degree that of Handel, either in his earlier or his later period."[1]   Macfarren, on the other hand maintained that the Magnificat "if not so mature, is perfectly congenial in style with all the more earnest compositions of Handel with which we are acquainted."[2]   In the presence of opposite judgments pronounced with equal confidence by recognized authorities, the appeal to the 'evidence of style' must be regarded—at any rate for the present—as indecisive.   There remains the reasonably probable hypothesis, based on external evidence, assigning it to Dionigi Erba—a hypothesis which the coming to light of other copies of the score or 'parts' might at any time conclusively establish—or refute.   Accordingly we are unable to say with certainty whether Handel, when incorporating practically the whole of this Magnificat in the second part of *Israel*, was appropriating a work by another composer or refurbishing one of his own.   I shall, therefore, in order not to prejudge this alternative, indicate the Magnificat in the sequel by the neutral abbreviation 'Mag.' rather than by the question-begging names 'Handel' or 'Erba,' though personally I am inclined to regard as preponderant the arguments against a Handelian origin for the disputed work.   For our immediate purpose, indeed, the question of authorship is unimportant, since, as has been seen, Handel's mode of dealing with earlier compositions of his own did not differ from that which he applied to those of other Masters.

The second Part of our oratorio opens with the majestic piece of choral declamation (No. 17) "Moses and the children of Israel," leading into the superbly jubilant double chorus (No. 18) "I will sing unto the Lord for He hath triumphed gloriously," in which no older material has been detected save, indeed, an ascending and descending scale passage, of four notes—a regular *locus communis* of contrapuntists—which Handel had used much less impressively in his Te Deum for the Peace of Utrecht in 1713.[3]

The duet for two Trebles (No. 19), "The Lord is my strength," which immediately follows this great effort, is simply a revised reproduction of a duet for the same voices in the *Magnificat*, accompanied too in the same manner, by unison violins with a practically unfigured bass in the oratorio, and by a viola with a figured bass in the *Magnificat*.   The comparison of the two settings is particularly instructive because it shows us Handel improving the earlier one exactly in the way in which a first-rate teacher of composition corrects the work of a promising pupil; cutting it about quite freely but without altering its essential character.   What strikes one as really surprising is that, considering the great amount of correction expended on what was after all only a moderately meritorious piece of work, Handel should not in this instance have preferred independent composition to so tiresome a process of adaptation.

---

[1] *Ib.* p. 173.   [2] Analysis of *Israel in Egypt* quoted by Chrysander.   *Ib.* p. 168. note.
[3] Chrysander : 'Life of Handel,' vol. I. p. 393.

In Ex. 35 and wherever the *Magnificat* is quoted in these pages Dr. Chrysander's edition is used; but I have omitted the figuring of the Bass as not required for the purposes of our comparison.

Ex. 35.

song,   The

strength   and   my   song,

H.   8   9

- ta - vit,

g.   7   8   9

et

H.

10 · · · · · · 11 · · · · · · 12

Lord is my strength and my song,———— and my song,————

The Lord is my strength and my song,———————— and my

Mag.

9 · · · · · · 10 · · · · · · 11

ex - ul - ta-vit, et ex - ul - ta-vit,

et ex - ul - ta-vit, et ex - ul -

H

H.   23   24   25

my sal-va-tion,

my sal-va-tion,

He is be -

Mag.   22

et ex - ul - ta-vit spi-ri-tus

Lord is my strength and my song, the Lord is my strength and my

strength and my song, the Lord is my strength and my song,

H. 30 31 32

ex - ul - ta - vit,

- ta - vit,

Mag. 28

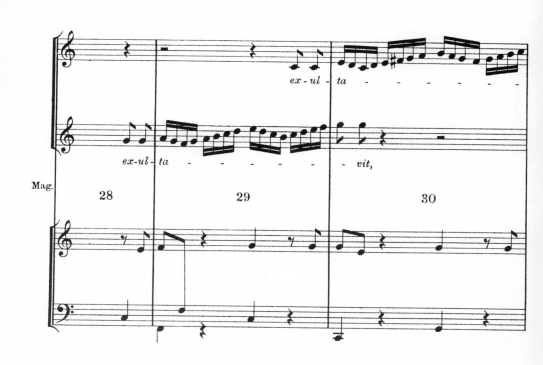

H.

35 36 37

- tion, my sal - va - tion, my sal - va - - - tion, He is be-come

my sal - va - - - - - tion, He is be-come my sal-

Mag.

31 32

- vit, ex - ul - ta - vit, ex - ul - ta - - - vit spi - ri-tus me - us

ex - ul - ta - - - - vit spi - ri-tus me - us in

my sal-va - - - - tion,

-va-tion, my sal-va - - - - tion, He is be-

H.   38   39   40

sa - lu - ta - - - ri me - o,   in

De - o sa - lu - ta - - - ri me - o,   in

Mag.   33   34   35

1st & 2nd Violins.
Viola & Bass.

The double chorus (No. 20) " He is my God," which comes next in order, consists of ten bars, of which the first two contain only percussions of the chord of A minor.   Bars 3-8, save for a slight alteration in bar 4, reproduce almost note for note the whole opening chorus of the *Magnificat*, and bars 9 and 10 contain the closing flash of genius which we have learned to expect from Handel when he has finished working up a piece of old material.   All this is shown in the following Example, in which I have not included the orchestral parts, as they possess no independent interest :

Ex. 36.

Passing over the chorus (No. 21) " And I will exalt him," which has not been shown to owe anything to pre-existing materials, we come to the famous duet for Two Basses, "The Lord is a man of war," in which Handel, besides making abundant use of a duet for the same voices in the *Magnificat*, has worked into the orchestral prelude and accompaniments a theme taken from a work by an earlier composer named Urio.

Of FRANCESCO ANTONIO URIO hardly anything appears to be known except that he was a priest and lived at Bologna in the seventeenth and beginning of the eighteenth centuries. The important fact for us is that he composed a *Te Deum* for voices and orchestra, a score of which, now in the Library of the Conservatoire at Paris, bears the heading "Te Deum, Urio, 1660."[1] Handel used this work very extensively in his *Dettingen Te Deum*,[2] and a theme from it, which had already done duty there, in the orchestral prelude to the chorus " All the earth doth worship Thee," leads off the introduction to "The Lord is a man of war," the rest of which is either directly copied from, or developed out of, the prelude to the duet in the *Magnificat*. This will be at once seen from the ensuing comparison, for the sake of which I have transposed the extract from Urio's *Te Deum* a Fourth down and that from the *Magnificat* a Minor Third down.

Ex. 37.

Handel. Symphony to "The Lord is a man of war."

Urio's Te Deum: Prelude to Chorus "*Te eternum*" (Transposed a Fourth down.)

[1] Grove, Dictionary of Music, 1st edition.

[2] A revised reprint, issued in 1902, of Chrysander's edition of Urio's *Te Deum* contains a preface describing the use made by Handel of that composition, which was absent from the earlier issue. (See above, Introd. pp. xi. and xii.)

Treble of bars 8 and 9 repeated a Fourth higher.

Bars 6 and 7 repeated with slight
alterations.

Urio's instr! phrase combined with vocal phrase from Magnificat treated in
canon.

No - men _____ sanc -

The duet proper opens with a phrase for the first Bass modelled on a lead for the vocal Altos in the *Dettingen Te Deum* chorus "All the earth doth worship Thee," where, as here, the Urio instrumental theme is used as accompaniment after having served as prelude.

Ex. 37. (continued.)

The next nineteen bars are made up of the same materials contrapuntally treated. Then comes a section 45 bars long in which the *Magnificat* is followed almost bar for bar:

Ex. 37. (continued.)

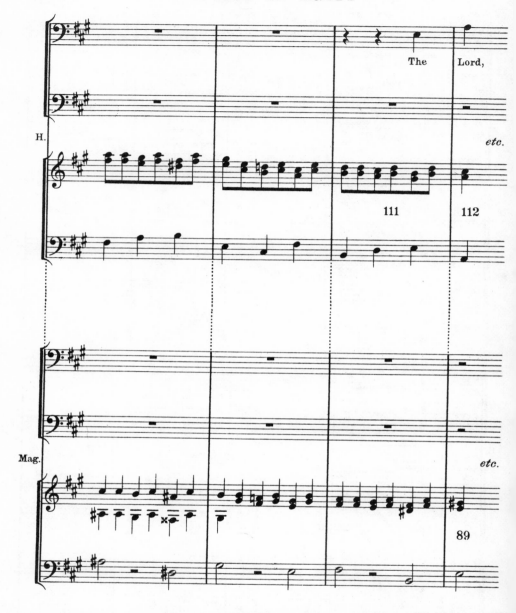

In bars 111 to 123 the two Basses sing successively a phrase beginning with that in bars 40 to 42 but lengthened by four bars, after which Handel works in a vocal phrase[1] of four bars with Urio accompaniment and then proceeds for the most part parallel with the *Magnificat* for 17 bars more:

[1] Which may itself have been taken from Urio's setting of "*Pleni sunt coeli*" but is too short to be definitely identified as borrowed.

Ex. 37. (continued.)

K

H.

in - to   the   sea.

in - to   the   sea.

etc.

men___ e -   jus.

men e -   jus.

Mag.

etc.

This section ends with bars 20-36 of the instrumental introduction repeated. Next come a few bars of vocal Canon leading to the fine descending Fifths on "also are drowned" which occur, fittingly set to "*misericordia*," in the *Magnificat*.

Ex. 37. (continued.)

This short passage is, after eight bars of other matter, repeated in the key of E major, and then Handel again takes up the thread of the *Magnificat* to form a famous passage:

Ex. 37. (continued.)

Handel purposes repeating this impressive passage with increased effect. Accordingly, in order to prepare a contrast for it, he takes the little subject already used in bars 124 and 125, adds to it a further bar of brisk quavers and works the result up into the following jubilant bit of canonic writing :

Ex. 37. (continued.)

The previous passage then comes in again, but this time in the key of A with the vocal parts in more sonorous positions in the Bass compass, and with the leading singer above, instead of, as before, below his colleague :

Ex. 37. (continued.)

This is the real close of the duet, for though a repetition of the opening symphony is directed to follow here, its effect, after the magnificent matter which has preceded it, is necessarily somewhat of an anti-climax. Handel's power of welding together heterogeneous materials into a perfectly homogeneous whole, imbued with a far grander spirit than dwelt in its original elements, can nowhere that I know of be seen at work with such unrelaxing energy as throughout this duet.

The next number (23), the double chorus "The depths have covered them," consists of sixteen bars, twelve of which are a reproduction, with quite astonishing improvements, of matter from a chorus in the *Magnificat*. In bars 1 and 2 Handel has provided some simple chords in the orchestra to fix the tonality, and in bars 3 and 4 has written vocal phrases congruent with those which he was about to transfer from the *Magnificat*.[1]

Ex. 38.

Choir I.

Handel.

Choir II.

Coro I.

Mag.

Coro II.

---

[1] See, for another instance of the latter procedure, bars 1-7 of "He spake the word." Ex. 27, p. 54.

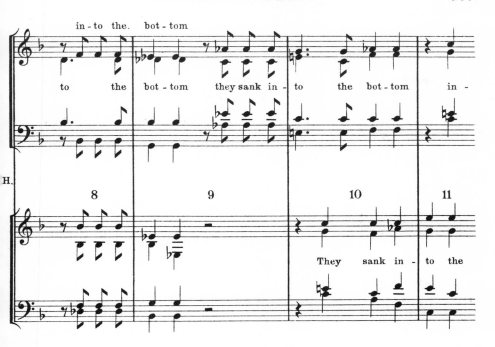

H.

14   15   16

co-ver'd them,   they sank in - to   the   bot-tom like a   stone.

they sank   in - to the bot-tom like a   stone.

Mag.

an - cil - lae   su - ae:

- cil - - - - lae   su - ae:

The next number (24), the double chorus, "Thy right hand, O Lord," opens as follows :

Ex. 39.

Thy right hand, O Lord, is become glo - rious in pow-er,

H.

is become glo - rious in pow-er, Thy right hand, O

Mag.

me dicent, di-cent

It will be observed that from the middle of bar 2 to the beginning of bar 5 Handel merely repeats the matter of bars 1 and half 2, slightly modified. He next, still following the *Magnificat*, takes the same subject into the key of G and, after a repetition similar to the former one, completes his use of this section of the *Magnificat*, which has now been entirely absorbed:

Ex. 39. (continued.)

is become glo - rious in pow-er, Thy right hand, O

H.   10   11   12

Thy right hand, O Lord, is become glo - rious in pow-er,

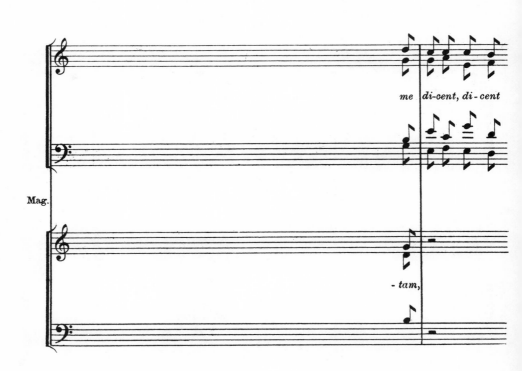

me di-cent, di-cent

Mag.

- tam,

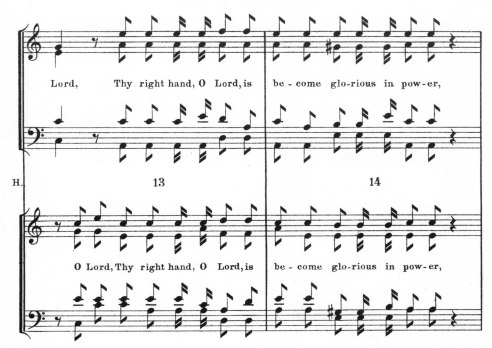

Lord, Thy right hand, O Lord, is be - come glo-rious in pow-er,

H. 13 14

O Lord, Thy right hand, O Lord, is be - come glo-rious in pow-er,

om-nes ge - ne - - - - ra - ti - o - - nes,

Mag.

om-nes ge - ne - - - - ra - ti - o - - nes,

The rest of this chorus is a fine specimen of Handel's contrapuntal powers. At bar 15 he starts a splendid subject:

Ex. 39. (continued.)

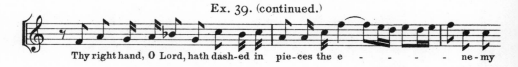

Thy right hand, O Lord, hath dash-ed in pie-ces the e - - - - ne-my

the first bar of which appears to have been developed from the bass of bar 1 of this section in the *Magnificat*. With this he makes play in Canon for half-a-dozen bars and then delivers again some of the earlier material, but greatly enriched, in a series of alternate utterances by the two choirs, which constantly increase in grandeur until they finally unite in the following prodigiously jubilant and exultant close:

Ex. 39. (continued.)

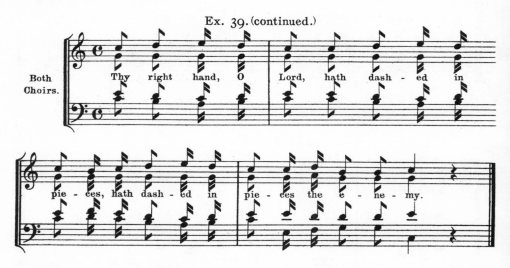

Both Choirs. Thy right hand, O Lord, hath dash - ed in pie - ces, hath dash - ed in pie - ces the e - ne - my.

Had the *Magnificat* not come down to us, the apparent complete spontaneity of this wonderful chorus would have at once negatived the idea that it could have been developed from a setting made to another text. There was, however, one indication pointing that way in the strong accent erroneously placed in this chorus on the first syllable of the word 'become' every time that it occurs. Nor could this be attributed to Handel's incomplete knowledge of English, for in the duet for two sopranos "The Lord is my strength"[1] where the word 'become' occurs far more frequently than in this chorus, it is invariably accentuated correctly.

A short choral introduction (No. 25), "And in the greatness of Thine excellency," leads into "Thou sentest forth Thy wrath which consumed them as

[1] See pp. 97-110.

stubble," a double chorus, 82 bars long, chiefly remarkable as being, with the exception of its last three bars, the entire choral setting in the *Magnificat* of the words "*Fecit potentiam in bracchio suo, dispersit superbos mente cordis sui,*" transferred bodily, with very few, and those quite insignificant, corrections, to the score of *Israel in Egypt*. The orchestral accompaniment, too, is taken over from that in the *Magnificat*, with parts for three trombones added to it, but substantially unchanged.

The three independent bars which Handel has appended by way of close present no point of interest.

This number is followed by the chorus (No. 27) "And with the blast" in which about 50 bars out of 71 are taken, or contrapuntally developed, from the Alto solo "*Deposuit potentes*" in the *Magnificat*. After one bar of orchestral prelude the chorus enters as shown in the following Example :

This Example shows Handel, after writing a couple of bars in Canon on an independent subject, taking up, and playing contrapuntally with, a phrase from the prelude in the *Magnificat*. He then modulates into the key of G and repeats the Canon there. Next he borrows a phrase from the song to which the prelude leads:

Ex. 40. (continued.)

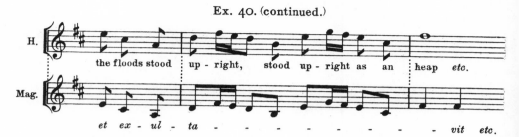

and occupies with it and a series of iterated crotchets the next twelve bars, after which he resumes continuous touch with his source as follows:

Ex. 40. (continued.)

The rest of the chorus is supplied by contrapuntal working on materials already used in it, more particularly on the groups of four notes descending by Thirds in the bass of the last extract from the *Magnificat*. With these Handel produces effects of wonderful sublimity which culminate at their last appearance just before the choral close:

Ex. 40. (continued.)

This is followed by twelve bars of concluding orchestral symphony closely modelled on those which perform the same function after the Alto solo in the *Magnificat*:

Ex. 40. (continued.)

The reader will observe that, whereas in bars 3 and 4 on page 152 Handel reaches five-part writing, he drops abruptly into three-part writing at the beginning of bar 5 and continues in it to the end of the movement.

A parallel drop from six-part to four-part writing occurs at the same place in ~~the~~ *Magnificat,* the stave in which parts for two oboes are written-in for the first three bars becoming abruptly vacant at the beginning of the fourth bar, and continuing so to the end of the symphony. Handel, however, does not silence his oboes, but directs them to play in unison with the first violin during the rest of the movement. In the *Magnificat* this symphony is also used as a prelude to the Alto solo, but with this difference that independent oboe-parts are there written-in throughout the ten bars of which it consists. The parts which Handel has discarded are certainly less interesting than that of the first violin, which he has improved and bidden the oboes to reinforce. This will be seen from the following Example :

Ex. 40. (continued.)

Passing over the two airs "The enemy said" and "Thou didst blow," and the double chorus "Who is like unto Thee," where there is no reason to suppose that Handel was indebted to any previous sources, we reach the double chorus (No. 31) "The earth swallowed them," which consists of 41 bars taken, as far as the voice parts are concerned, all but note for note from the setting in the *Magnificat* of "*Sicut erat in principio*" etc.

The false accentuation on 'The' in bar 1

Ex. 41.

might, even without access to the *Magnificat*, have raised a suspicion that the setting here was not absolutely original.

The Alto and Tenor duet, "Thou in Thy mercy," is almost wholly based on a composition for the same voices in the *Magnificat* set to the words "*Esurientes implevit bonis.*" Out of the 115 bars which this movement occupies in *Israel*, only 26 appear to owe nothing to the *Magnificat*, and 17 more to contain a mixture of independent and derived matter. But the improvement effected on the material taken over, especially by supplying an interesting string accompaniment where the *Magnificat* had only a bare figured bass, is very great.

The duet in the *Magnificat* not being provided with an instrumental symphony, Handel has supplied one, the first half of which is made out of its opening vocal subject, and the second half appears to have been scored independently, as will be seen in the next Example:

Ex. 42.

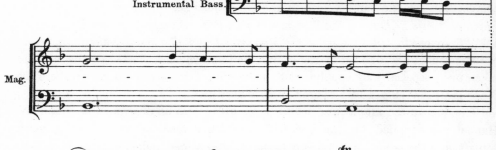

The duet then proceeds side by side in the two versions for many bars, as the next Example will show. The first five bars from ~~the~~ *Magnificat* already quoted are repeated here for convenience of comparison.

Ex. 42. (continued.)

Handel constructs the next five bars by repeating the last five, transposed a Fifth higher, and with the voice-parts inverted :

Ex. 42. (continued.)

M

After a short instrumental interlude, abridged from the opening symphony to this duet, Handel leads off a section not taken from ~~the~~ *Magnificat*, beginning with the beautiful phrase :

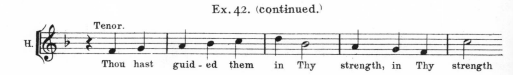

Ex. 42. (continued.)

This he first works contrapuntally for the voices, and then modifies, while ingeniously constructing an instrumental accompaniment for it out of the vocal material of the duet, as shown in the following Example :

Ex. 42. (continued.)

A complete repetition of the introductory symphony terminates the duet.

The succeeding number (33) is the colossal double chorus, "The people shall hear," probably the greatest of all Handel's polyphonic compositions, and certainly one which both as respects construction and sublimity has been surpassed by the choral masterpieces of J. S. Bach alone. Fortunately there is no ground for doubting that it is a thoroughly spontaneous product of his genius. Dr. Chrysander has, it is true, suggested that a morsel from Stradella's Serenata may have given Handel the first germ of his wonderful setting of "shall melt away."[1] The passages in question open thus :

---

[1] See the table of contents prefixed to his edition of the Serenata.

Ex. 43.

Choir I. — Handel.

shall melt a - way

shall melt a - way

Choir II.

shall melt a - way

Instr. Bass.

shall melt

Soprano. Stradella. Serenata p. 24, (Transposed a Tone up.) Instrumental Bass.

A - mi - che, a - mi - che a pie - tà

Ne mi - che, ne mi - che a pie - tà

Bass.

Instr. Bass.

but the resemblance is evidently too slight to prove anything.

This terminates our survey of *Israel in Egypt*, as its remaining matter (Nos. 34-39) contains nothing relevant to our present inquiry, indeed mainly consists in the repetition, with some additions, of the double chorus (No. 18) which, with No. 17, opens Part II. of the oratorio.

CHAPTER VIII.

DISCUSSION OF THE QUESTION WHETHER HANDEL'S MODE OF DEALING WITH COMPOSITIONS BY OTHER MASTERS WAS MORALLY JUSTIFIABLE.

IN our survey of parallel passages contained in Chapters V. and VI. we saw by numerous instances that Handel was in the habit of working up his own earlier compositions into new forms. In this he was, indeed, only following the practice of his time, even when, as we saw him doing in movements in the *Messiah,* he divorced music which he had previously written to extremely secular words and reset it to others of a strongly sacred character. It may interest my readers to see his great contemporary, John Sebastian Bach, doing exactly the same thing in his *Dramma per Musica* "The choice of Hercules" and his *Christmas Oratorio.* The former work contains a song in which 'Pleasure' lulls Hercules to sleep with the advice to "follow the allurements of raging desire, revel in enjoyment and recognize no bounds." The music to this reappears, substantially unaltered, as the celebrated cradle-song in the *Christmas Oratorio.* Again, Hercules, in a vigorous aria, proclaims his refusal to listen to "abandoned Pleasure," and boasts that he has "long since crushed and torn to pieces the serpents that sought to catch him in their toils." Save for a few alterations, the music set to these denunciatory words is that of the Alto song in the *Christmas Oratorio* calling on Zion to prepare herself to receive with tender endearments the infant Messiah. Admirers of that song have doubtless wondered, as I have, why in its second part a moving bass with an undulating effect is introduced, though there is nothing in the praises of Zion's beauty, which form the text, to suggest such treatment. Inspection of the next Example will show that this accompaniment was, in the earlier form of the composition, an imitation of snake-motion, which, by simple transference, has come to occupy an inappropriate place in the *Christmas Oratorio.*[1]

Ex. 44.

Alto.

Christmas Oratorio: *Dei-ne Wan - gen müs-sen heut' viel schö - ner pran - gen*
Choice of Hercules: *Denn die Schlan-gen die mich woll - ten wie - gend fan - gen* etc

Instr!
Bass.

Comparisons such as the above and those which we have already made between settings by Handel of secular words and their employment in the *Messiah*[2] are at

---

[1] My attention was first drawn to the connexion between the *Christmas Oratorio* and the *Dramma per Musica* by that excellent Bach scholar, Mr. Donald Tovey.   [2] Pages 36-46.

first sight rather perturbing, but have their use in reminding us that music is not in itself either 'sacred' or 'secular.' It may, when set to sacred or secular words, gather to itself their respective associations: it may be grave or light in character, and so better fitted for the one destination than for the other. But, as religious emotion does not differ in essence from secular emotion of a kindred sort, music, however splendidly adapted for association with either, can *express* neither as distinguished from the other. Such, however, is the strength of association, that at the present day no leading composer would venture on transferences such as those we have seen effected by Handel and Bach. Nor is the reason of this difference far to seek, residing, as it does, in the vast extension of music-publishing since the days of those great men.

To us, who are apt to consider that an injury is done us if we cannot buy a pianoforte score of a great choral work for a shilling or two, it seems at first sight incredible that, in spite of Handel's enormous popularity, only *one* of his compositions of that class, *Alexander's Feast*, was published in a complete form during his life-time, the oratorios having appeared only in selections with the choruses left out.[1] Of Bach's church cantatas, also, only one[2] attained publication during his life, and that, perhaps, less on account of its intrinsic merit than because it was composed to celebrate an election of town-councillors.[3] The rest of his compositions of that class, and they numbered hundreds, remained in manuscript at his death. Now the fact of publication or no publication would evidently greatly affect a composer's attitude towards his works. If he had *published* a setting of a particular text, his music had thereby entered into a union with it for better for worse, a printed certificate of which was producible at any moment. But if the setting had *not* been published, the composer occupied a freer position, and by attaching his music to new texts might secure further hearings for it—assuredly a legitimate object of ambition. We may thus explain, *e.g.*, Bach's incorporation in the Mass in B minor of materials already used in his church cantatas, and Handel's manifold adaptations from his own older choral compositions in *Israel in Egypt* and elsewhere. Even in the case of settings transferred from light secular to decidedly religious texts, the fact of non-publication prevented any fixed association growing up between music and words such as would make a fresh destination given to the former appear incongruous or even lacking in reverence.

Enough has, I think, now been said on Handel's readaptations of his own old materials, in which he followed what was the practice, and, as I have tried to show, a not unreasonable practice, of his age. His appropriations from the works of other composers, living and dead, went, on the contrary, both as to their character and their extent, far beyond anything that has been established, or even asserted,

---

[1] Chrysander's 'Life of Handel,' vol. II., pp. 428, 429.   [2] "*Gott ist mein König.*"
[3] Sedley Taylor, 'Life of Bach:' Cambridge, Macmillan and Bowes, 1897, p. 25.

in the case of any other composer of the first rank. They give rise to a problem of remarkable interest and no small difficulty, viz., how it was that Handel, who is recognised on all hands as having been a thoroughly honourable man, can have thought himself at liberty to take such unprecedented liberties with the results of other men's labours. But before entering on the discussion of this problem, let us try to ascertain at what period of his career specimens of this method of procedure first show themselves.

It is well known that Handel's only teacher in music was Zachau (or to adopt the correct spelling, Zachow), the principal organist at Halle, under whose instruction he remained from early boyhood until he was qualified to start as an independent musician. As Zachow was a somewhat prolific composer, it seemed a not unreasonable conjecture that when his works came to be published they would prove to have been a further quarry of Handelian ideas. Their recent appearance under the editorship of Dr. Max Seiffert[1] has, however, failed to verify this forecast. A few instances of parallel treatment and similarity of phrase present themselves and have been pointed out by Dr. Seiffert, but none of thematic appropriation such as Handel subsequently practised. Nor need this surprise us, for Zachow's melodies were too dull and his harmonies too common-place to have stirred the emancipated Handel to thoughts of appropriation. But, for all that, Dr. Seiffert has ably shown[2] that Zachow was a thoroughly equipped church musician of a sound pre-Bachian type, who at the time when Handel was under his charge was himself actively endeavouring to advance in his art, and is therefore likely to have given the young genius exactly the kind of instruction best suited for his future development. Handel is known to have always spoken of his one and only teacher in music with the utmost respect, and through Dr. Seiffert's exertions we know in some measure why he did so.

In 1703 Handel, then in his eighteenth year, went to Hamburg, where he occupied, until 1706, a post as violinist and accompanist at the harpsichord in the orchestra of the opera, at that time one of the first in Europe. His contemporary and associate, Matheson, has left us the following account of Handel's powers on his arrival at Hamburg:

"He used at that time to compose very long, long Arias and almost endless Cantatas, which yet had neither the right skill nor the right taste, though they possessed a complete harmony, but the high school of opera soon fashioned him into something quite different. . . . . ."

"He was strong on the organ: stronger than Kuhnau[3] in fugues and counter-points, especially extempore, but he knew very little of melody before he had to do

---

[1] *Denkmäler deutscher Tonkunst*, Bde 21, 22. 1905.

[2] In the preface to his edition of Zachow's works and more at large in an unpublished Paper which he has very kindly allowed me to see in manuscript.

[3] J. S. Bach's immediate predecessor at the Leipzig *Thomasschule*.

with the Hamburg operas. . . . During the last [seventeenth] century, hardly anybody thought of melody ; harmony was the one and only object aimed at." [1]

REINHARD KEISER (1673-1739), the director and leading composer of the Hamburg opera during Handel's time there, is described by Chrysander[2] as a man whose morality was "equal to zero," and who was by no means remarkable for his acquirements in technical musicianship, but endowed by nature with a seemingly inexhaustible spring of beautiful ideas whence he poured out incessantly during forty years a stream of some hundred-and-twenty operas. We must think, then, of Handel as gathering, in this school, ideas concerning the formation of melody. Dr. Max Seiffert, in the preface to the edition of Keiser's opera *Octavia* which forms No. 6 of the Handel 'Supplements,'[3] gives us the opportunity of observing this process at closer quarters, as will be seen by the following passage which I translate thence :

"Keiser had in the year 1704 begun to set "Almira" and finished some of it, but then, in the rush and turmoil of operatic management, had let the work drop and at last handed over the libretto by way of experiment to the young Handel, whose setting met with so warm a reception by the Hamburgers that, between the 8th of January and the 25th of February, 1705, it was given 19 or 20 times running. Handel strengthened the good impression which his first opera had made by at once following it up with a second, "Nero." Its first performance took place on Feb. 25, thus interrupting the long run of "Almira;" and, as "Nero" also made a success, Handel had the pleasure of hearing his own music performed continuously until the beginning of Lent, during which theatrical performances were forbidden. This success of the novice in opera caused the utmost annoyance to Keiser, who forthwith set to work to compose the same dramatic materials himself. In the following August he brought on the stage his "Octavia," which displaced Handel's "Nero," and his "Almira" followed it later. Beside this Keiser sent to press a selection of the most beautiful Arias and Recitatives in his "Almira" and "Octavia" with the purpose of challenging a comparison between his compositions and those of Handel. . . . . Handel took no notice of all this, and, moreover, the opera-intrigues led at that time to an abrupt disappearance of Keiser from Hamburg. Handel, too, quitted the town at the end of 1706 in order to go to Italy ; but he retained Keiser's proceedings in his memory in order on a fitting occasion to inflict an innocent requital for them.

"Among the German music which Handel took with him on his journey was a manuscript score of Keiser's "Octavia." To study it seriously and work it up exhaustively as a source for his own activity, was the form which his requital took. Everything in the way of reminiscences of Keiser's melodies which we find in Handel's Italian compositions points back to "Octavia.""

---

[1] Quoted by Chrysander, 'Life of Handel,' vol. I., p. 85.   [2] Ibidem, p. 80.
[3] Leipzig, Handel Society, 1902.

Dr. Seiffert follows up these remarks by specifying ten phrases in "Octavia" one or more of which reappear in operatic and other works of Handel belonging to the years 1707, 1708, 1714 and 1715. The very popular opera *Agrippina* contains six of these phrases: one of them appears in three works, six occur in two each and three in one each. I will set out four of these belonging to the years 1707 and 1708, as they supply materials for interesting comparisons showing Handel thus early in his career employing, on a small scale, the same system which he carried out, on so great an one, in later years.

Ex. 45.

From a setting of *"Laudate pueri"* (Rome, 1707.)

From an aria in *Octavia*.

Ex. 46.

Symphony to the song *"Dell' Iberia al soglio."* (*Rodrigo,* Handel's first *Italian* opera, Florence 1707.)

Handel.
(*Rodrigo.*)

Symphony to the song *"Es streiten mit reizender Blüthe."* (*Octavia.*)

Keiser.
p. 84.
Transposed
one Tone
down.

H.

K.

2 bars omitted.

H.

K.

Ex. 47.

From a song sung by 'Lucifer' in Handel's cantata *"La Resurrezione"*(Rome, 1708.)

Handel.
(*Resurrezione.*)

O voi dell' E - re _ bo   po - ten _ ze or _ ri _ bi _ li

Bass of Symphony to the song *"Costante ognor."* (Octavia.)

Keiser.
(*Octavia.*)
p. 147.
(Transposed
a Tone down.)

sù,   me - co ar - ma - te - vi   d'i - ra e   va - lor

Ex. 48.

Symphony to the song *"Vaghe Fonte."* (*Agrippina*, 1708.)

Handel.
Agrippina.

Symphony to the song *"Ruhig sein."*

Keiser.
Octavia.
p. 12.
(Transposed
a Tone
down.)

Except for the obligations to Keiser which have been named above,[1] nothing appears to have been found to show that Handel in the long series of his Italian

[1] See p. 168.

operas made any important use of extraneous sources.   But the examples set out in the present volume suffice to show that in the series of choral works composed between 1737 and 1757 he drew on such sources pretty continuously.   The names of the works in which we have seen him doing this stand as follows in chronological order :

Trionfo del Tempo, - - - - - - - - -	1737
Israel in Egypt, - - - - - - - - -	1738
Ode for St. Cecilia's Day, - - - - - - -	1739
Samson, - - - - - - - - - -	1741
Dettingen Te Deum, - - - - - - - -	1743
Joshua, - - - - - - - - - -	1747
Theodora, - - - - - - - - - -	1749
Jephtha, - - - - - - - - - -	1751
Triumph of Time and Truth, - - - - - -	1757

In 1752 the disease in Handel's eyes began, which, after three couchings, left him totally blind.   This calamity fully accounts for the cessation of production between *Jephtha* and the *Triumph of Time and Truth,* which latter was mainly made up of older work and constituted his final effort.

That Handel appropriated consciously and deliberately would, I think, be clear even if we possessed no other evidence than that supplied by comparison of passages.   The similarities are much too minute and extensive to be accounted for either by fortuitous coincidence or by unconscious reminiscence.   The former explanation would demand a series of gigantic improbabilities, the latter a combination of superhuman memory of music with infrahuman forgetfulness of authorship.   But the evidence supplied by the Fitzwilliam autographs removes any shadow of doubt remaining on this point.   They constitute what is in effect Handel's common-place book into which he copied from works by other composers passages ranging from short phrases to entire long movements, many of which he subsequently incorporated, sometimes with much, sometimes with very slight, alteration, in his autograph scores.

We must therefore, I think, conclude that Handel's procedure was deliberate and thoroughly systematic.   But before approaching the personal issues which this conclusion opens, it is necessary to consider the question whether public opinion in Handel's time regarded the unacknowledged appropriation of other men's musical ideas in the light in which it would be regarded now.   Fortunately for us a correspondence which took place in 1731 and was published in the following year[1] throws a most instructive light on this question.

[1] "Letters from the Academy of Ancient Musick at London, to Sig^r. Antonio Lotti of Venice : with his Answers and Testimonies.   London : Printed by Geo. James.   MDCCXXXII."

I owe the perusal of this extremely rare pamphlet to the kindness of the Librarian of the Faculty of Advocates' Library at Edinburgh, who most obligingly sent the volume containing it to the custody of the University Library, Cambridge, for my benefit.   Dr. Chrysander (Life of Handel, vol. II. pp. 293-297) and Victor Schœlcher (Life of Handel, pp. 149-155) have both quoted extracts from these letters.

On Feb. 5, 1731, Mr. Howley Bishop, Secretary of the Academy of Ancient Music, addressed, by order of that body, a letter written both in English and Latin, to Signor Lotti at Venice, in which, after a few introductory paragraphs describing the scope and character of the Academy's work he came to the gist of his communication in the following terms: " One of our Members having received from *Venice* a Book entitled *Duetti, &c.,* and having look'd it over, pitch'd upon the XVIII. Madrigal, the only one for five Voices, inscribed *La Vita Caduca,* beginning *In una Siepe,* to be performed in the Academy. Signor *Buononcini,* who is also one of our Members, and who three or four years before had presented us this very Madrigal as his own, being inform'd of this, immediately sent a letter to the Academy, in which having greatly complained of the Person who introduced it among us under your Name, he accuses you as the Plagiary of his Works, and affirms that he composed this Madrigal thirty years ago, exactly as it is printed in your Book, at the command of the Emperor *Leopold;* and for the Proof of this appeals to the archives of that Emperor."

After saying that he had also, by order of the Academy, applied for information to " *M. Fuchs,* Chappel-Master to the Emperor," Bishop added: " I don't therefore in the least doubt but that you will have so much Regard for your own Fame and Reputation among us, as to inform us as soon as possibly you can how this Matter stands."

To this direct and characteristically British appeal Lotti replied in a French letter dated Venice, March 29, 1731. After some courteous introductory remarks about the Academy he continued:

"Touching the object of your letter I confess the truth to you, Sir, when I say that I was extremely surprised to see myself accused of being the debtor of my own property, and after twenty-six years that my book has been in the hands of the public, to find myself obliged to prove that it belongs to me. If this had been represented to me from any other quarter, I should have appealed to the public notoriety of the fact and have intrenched myself in silence; but the esteem which I owe to yourself, and to the illustrious body whom you represent, calls on me to satisfy your request."

Lotti goes on to do this by saying that the Duetti, Terzetti, and Madrigals were composed by him shortly before their publication and that there were professional musicians and amateurs who had witnessed the progress of the disputed madrigal and taken part, some as singers and some as hearers, when it was rehearsed from the rough draft before being written out fair. Further that the words of it had been specially written for and given to him by the Abbé Periati, who was then at Vienna, where the Madrigal was performed before the Emperor Leopold.

After mentioning these and a few more evidences of his authorship, Lotti begs the Secretary to be on his guard "lest, in order to do a bad turn to M. Buononcini, some one had falsely attributed to him the letter written in his name to the

Academy, because it is incredible that, learned musician as he is, he should have been willing, out of light-heartedness, to adopt my defects as his own."

The next move was a communication dated April 14, 1731, from the Secretary addressed by order of the Academy to Signor Buononcini, enclosing copies of the letters to and from Signor Lotti. "The Academy," he wrote, "thought themselves obliged in Justice to acquaint you with what he says in Support of his own Claim and in opposition to yours. I have therefore omitted a Post in returning him an Answer, that I might have an opportunity of receiving your Commands in relation to any thing you shall think proper for me to say in my Reply. I shall wait till the middle of next Week in Expectation of the Favour of a Letter from you. . ."

The non-result of this application is shown in a second letter to Signor Lotti dated June 5, 1731, which had been delayed by a prolonged illness of the Secretary. It begins by informing him that the Academy unanimously agreed that the Madrigal was his, and continues thus :

" I also (which we thought just) wrote a letter to Signor *Buononcini*, which was delivered into his own Hands, in which I sent him copies of both our letters, and told him I would wait a Week before I wrote to you again, that he might, if he should think proper, have an opportunity of replying. But I waited a Fortnight to no Purpose. I then sent a second Letter by the Keeper of our Library, and Signor *Buononcini* not being at home two or three times, I order'd it to be left with his Servant; but this also, which I am surprised at, was denied : For the Servant said he had Orders to receive no Letters but what came by the Post. Thus stands the affair with Signor *Buononcini*. Yet notwithstanding this, some Persons who pretend to be his Friends, and who have separated from the Academy on this very Account, as it appears since no other is pretended, obstinately assert the Madrigal to be his, still appeal to the Archives of the Emperor, and accuse you of Theft, and the Academy of Slander through the whole Town. No answer from M. *Fuchs* has yet come to my Hands, from what Cause or by what Accident, if he be still alive, I can't so much as guess. The Academy, after hearing your Letter were willing to have prosecuted this Affair no farther, but they think it is your Interest as well as theirs, that these Calumnies should be answered. They intreat therefore, Sir, that entirely to refute these ill-minded Persons, you would be pleased to send us some Certificates of the Count *de Par*, Abbot *(sic)* Periati, or some others who saw the Madrigal at *Venice* before it was published."

The letter ends with a request to Signor Lotti that he would allow his name to be entered on the list of Members of the Academy. Lotti's reply—this time written in Italian—is so very charming that, though it is rather long, I cannot resist reproducing it almost in full.

" I have received, Illustrious Sir, your most gracious letter of June 5 and, much as the news of your ill health grieved me, so on the other hand was I equally consoled by that of its complete re-establishment. I thank you, the whole

Academy and the worthy Members who compose it, for the justice they do me, and may God grant, since they agree as to the Author of the Madrigal, that they may also be able to agree in their approval of the work itself.   I hear how Partisans of Sign. Buononcini are out of temper with the Academy and with me, and I could wish I possessed the art of that lost Music which excited and calmed the Passions. I think too that they little consult the glory of their Friend, because, by withdrawing themselves on this account from the Academy they exhibit a degree of anger which would be just had an only Son[1] been concerned, but is after all excessive for a Madrigal, when Sign. Buononcini can make similar madrigals and better ones too.   At Venice, on the contrary, and at Vienna, all is quiet, indeed my friends joke with me about a composition of mine having been set up in the arena as if it had been the Golden apple the possession of which was to be contended for. As for the certificates asked of me, I verily should have thought I stood in no need of this remedy, as I am in good health ; but I ought to submit myself to the opinion and command of the Academy ; I therefore enclose some papers from Vienna and from Venice, sufficient even for any one who hates the Truth.   I consigned to Mr. Smith,[2] three months ago, in accordance with your command and with the courage which it gave me, some of my musical things, which shall be followed by others, and among these you will find a Madrigal for 5 voices, which I composed at Dresden, during the time that I was in the service of that Court, and you will recognize that it is Grist from the same Mill.   I know not whether this will have the fate of being attributed to any one else ; in which case I shall equally console myself, with the reflection that my parts are not judged so indifferent when they meet with people who wish to adopt them as their own.   But let us make an end, Illustrious Sir, of this ridiculous business which was not set going by us, into which I entered for obedience' sake, and from which, as I do not fear shame, so I claim no glory.   Let us pass on to better things.   A more laudable, a more profitable, a more grateful, study the Academy could not set before itself and as far as my forces will permit, they will always have in me an admirer and a disciple of the sublime models which Antiquity has left us, among which it will be extremely agreeable and instructive to me to be able to see the works of old *English* composers which you offer me with so much courtesy."

The rest of the letter contains only expressions of gratitude towards the Academy.   The accompanying certificates consist of affidavits made by leading

---

[1] An amusing blunder in the version of this sentence given in Schœlcher's ' Life of Handel,' p. 153, makes Lotti write that Buononcini's partisans showed a resentment which might be just were the dispute about " an *air* only," but was excessive for a madrigal.   Lotti's words are " *un Figlio unico*," which Schœlcher, who wrote in French, would of course translate " *un fils unique* " and his English translator may have rendered " an only heir."   It needed but the thoughtless attentions of some proof-reader to " correct " this into " an air only " and thereby reduce Lotti's sensible remark to sheer nonsense.   [2] British Consul at Venice.

musicians at Venice and Vienna : they constitute overwhelming proof of Lotti's claim to be the composer of the Madrigal.

The correspondence ends with an undated letter addressed to Signor Lotti by the Directors of the Academy in person, the Secretary being disabled by illness from discharging his official functions. After some preliminary matter they write :

" The testimonies, dear Sir, you transmitted to us, have had their due Weight with us, and abundantly confirm us in the good Opinion we had before conceived of you. It can be no disagreeable News to you to hear that we have sent them, together with the several letters that have passed between us, to be printed. This Procedure will serve eternally to convince you of our good and sincere Intentions towards you ; and at the same time confound those who have taken upon them to arraign our conduct throughout this affair. We will take care you shall have some of the printed copies by the first opportunity. By the ship called the *Ruby*, you will receive from us two Pieces of Musick, the Work of two *English* Masters, *Tho. Tallis* and *William Bird*, the latter organist and composer to Henry VIII., the former Master of the Royal Chapel in the Reign of the same King. When you cast your Eye upon those Pieces, you will clearly perceive that true and solid Musick is not in its Infancy with us, and that, whatever some on your Side of the *Alps* may imagine to the contrary, the Muses have of old time taken up their abode in *England*."

The letter is signed

Directors of the Academy
{
John Pelling, *S.T.P.*
Hen. Needler, *Philomus.*
Humphry Wyrley, *Philomus.*
J. C. Pepusch, *Doctor of Musick.*
Bernard Gates, *Master of the children of his Majesty's chappel.*
J. Freeman, *one of the Gentlemen of his Majesty's chappel.*
}

This correspondence shows conclusively that plagiarism was regarded by educated musicians in the eighteenth century exactly as it is regarded by them in the twentieth. A charge of being a " Plagiary " is what no man who has " regard for his own fame and reputation " can afford to leave unrebutted. To impute plagiarism is to impute " theft," and the imputation, if untrue, is " slander " and " calumny." And that public opinion viewed the matter in the same light is shown by the fact that when, through the publication of the correspondence, the conduct of Buononcini had become generally known, his adherents withdrew their support, his principal patrons, the Marlborough family, severed their connexion with him, and he finally found himself practically obliged to leave the country.[1]

The same correspondence affords firm ground from which to approach another

---

[1] Article in Grove's Dictionary, 2nd edition.

question which now presents itself:—Was the fact of Handel's indebtedness to other composers, living and dead, at all generally known during his life-time? If so, it is hardly conceivable that the powerful party known to have been so furiously and relentlessly hostile to Handel should have one and all abstained from using against him the weapon—a charge of plagiarism—to be convicted of which had proved so ruinous to his former rival, Buononcini. That such a charge was not made by them appears certain from the silence of subsequent historians about it, and from the claim to absolute originality which they put forth, as we have seen,[1] on Handel's behalf.

But it may be maintained that the term 'plagiarism' is totally inapplicable to Handel's appropriations which had so immensely improved and glorified the appropriated material that, even supposing them to have been contemporaneously notorious, no charge of plagiarism could with any hope of success have been brought against him. This view, which was that of Dr. Chrysander,[2] has been stated in the following terms by Dr. Max Seiffert:[3]

"During Handel's lifetime he had opponents and enviers enough: all their machinations, however, produced but a passing effect—Handel always got the upper hand again with new deeds and works, compelling admiration by his art. His treatment of the works of other Masters could not at that time remain unnoticed: the works were for the most part accessible in print and played a part in musical life. There were also enough connoisseurs who could have raised effective protest against the illegitimate use of other people's property, and have branded as such Handel's dishonourable proceeding. Nothing of the kind happened. Surely the only conclusion to be drawn from this fact is that Handel's contemporaries found nothing to blame in his procedure."

Expanding a hint given by Heinichen on the subject of musical plagiarism in general,[4] Seiffert lays down as follows the conditions the presence of which renders that term inapplicable:

"Before one can speak of a plagiarism, it is necessary to examine whether the foreign ideas in their original connexion are literally taken over, or whether they are differently combined or submitted to fresh harmonic treatment, melodic development and contrapuntal interweaving. In the latter case the independence of the composer counts as assured. This exactly hits Handel's case."

On this argumentation I have two criticisms to offer:

1. While some among the works of which Handel made free use, e.g. Muffat's

---

[1] See *Introduction*, pp. ix, x.

[2] " While Handel took possession quite notoriously (*offenkundig*) of so much extraneous material, without any one daring to call him to account, his rival [Buononcini] has, curiously enough, to serve as the means of making us recognize the difference between thievish and legitimate transference." Life of Handel. Vol. II. p. 302.   [3] *Kirchenmusikalisches Jahrbuch*, 1903. p. 93.

[4] " *Ich suche in dergleichen Dubiis etwas in der Arte Combinatoria.*" Heinichen: ' *Der Generalbass in der composition*,' Dresden, 1728 p. 33, quoted by Seiffert, *Ibidem.*

N

Componimenti, were accessible in print in his time, Dr. Seiffert goes, I think, a little beyond what the facts warrant in saying that this was the case with these works " for the most part." Several of those from which Handel borrowed most largely, composed by Stradella, Urio, Graun and Habermann, were certainly not in print at that time. But even if they had been, this would not have necessarily led to a general knowledge of Handel's appropriations, for lack of the other term of the comparison, as his choruses, to which he transferred most of the borrowed materials, were, with the single exception named above,[1] not published during his life-time. To detect and hunt down to some extraneous source a passage which one had only heard in performance, and could not consult a score of, would involve an effort possible only to exceptionally tenacious memories. These considerations go far towards explaining how Handel's methods may have remained unsuspected by his contemporaries.

2. That there is often the greatest originality in the forms into which borrowed materials were worked up by Handel is indisputable, and has been amply proved in the present volume. But that infuriated opponents would have been withheld by such refined distinctions as those laid down by Seiffert from charging Handel with plagiarism, had they been acquainted with such transferences as those from Stradella and Kerl in *Israel in Egypt*, or from Graun in *The Triumph of Time and Truth*—to mention only these—appears to me incredible. So far, therefore, as the evidence before us goes, it points, I think, to the conclusion that, if no contemporary voice was raised against Handel's annexations, this was because they were not publicly recognised as such during his life-time.

Be this as it may, however, thus much is indisputable—that Handel, though he apparently never acknowledged his sources, was yet far from acting as if he thought he had anything to fear from their detection and exposure. He laid under contribution works by distinguished contemporaries as freely as those of forgotten predecessors. Thus we have seen him inserting, in operas of 1707 and 1708, phrases taken from Keiser's *Octavia* composed in 1705. From his contemporaries Muffat, Habermann and Graun, who all outlived him, he borrowed very deliberately. The retribution which fell on his old rival Buononcini, in 1732,[2] can have had no terrors for Handel, who, only five years later, incorporated in his *Trionfc del Tempo* (1737) two entire choruses taken almost unchanged from a work by Graun. In the English *Triumph of Time and Truth* (1757), which was his last work, he not only repeated one of these choruses, but proceeded to appropriate, though with additions and manifest improvements, a chorus from a mass by Antonio Lotti (+1740), the very man from whom Buononcini, with results so disastrous to himself, had sought to filch the credit due for the composition of the madrigal "*In una siepe ombrosa*"! This final act of annexation, to which notice

---

[1] See p. 165.   [2] See p. 176.

has not hitherto, as far as I am aware, been publicly called, was recognised by Dr. Crotch (+1847) with the aid of Latrobe's 'Selection of Sacred Music,' which contains a "Qui Tollis from a Mass by Antonio Lotti." In some manuscript notes by Crotch in a copy of the *Triumph of Time and Truth* belonging to the British Museum he has written against a passage in the chorus "Comfort them, O Lord" the words "This passage all from Lotti—in Latrobe No. 16." Mr. Barclay Squire very kindly drew my attention to these notes by Crotch,[1] and my friend Mr. A. M. Hind was good enough to copy for me the extract from Latrobe[2] which is set out in the following comparison. The accompaniment described by Latrobe as for the cembalo [*i.e.* harpsichord] is no doubt arranged from an orchestral accompaniment in Lotti's mass, the original form of which I have not seen.

Ex. 49.

Chorus from *"The Triumph of Time and Truth."*

[1] Another entry in these notes shows that Crotch had anticipated Mr. Lunn in recognizing the identity of the chorus "To dust his glory" in *The Triumph of Time and Truth* with that published as Graun's by Latrobe. See above pp. 31, 32.   [2] Vol. II. p. 62.

bed   in   sickness! Comfort them, make Thou   their   bed,

Accompaniment,
string parts only.

no - bis!   mi - se - re -   - re,

Cembalo.

It will be observed here how Handel from his fifteenth bar onwards improves the effect by putting the treble of Lotti's accompaniment into the mouths of his own sopranos.

In trying to form an idea what was Handel's object in adopting the procedure which he carried out so extensively and systematically, we shall do well to begin by examining the views which have been put forth on this subject by Dr. Chrysander. He sets out by asking somewhat indignantly, in reference to a remark made by Schœlcher, an earlier biographer of Handel, whether "anything more disgraceful can be attributed to a composer than that he seeks to enrich himself illegitimately at the cost of his fellows?" and continues : "If the treatment of the whole question had started with an examination of how Handel made use of the Magnificat for *Israel* and *Susanna*, it would indeed have been shown, independently of all external proofs, that he did not compose the work, but his relation to it would also have appeared in a quite different aspect. In the course of this transformation things come to light which are completely new and so overwhelming that an observer finds it difficult to preserve the requisite balance during the investigation. What he retained note-for-note, and what in unexpected fashion he created entirely new, all has become his own. How great Handel is and what a commanding position he occupies towards other musicians becomes thoroughly palpable only through work of this kind. If sufficient insight has been gained into the relation here set before us the idea of robbery cannot present itself, and not less certain is it that it was not arrogance which drove him to such rearrangement. It was the impulse of his artistic nature to save from perishing musical ideas which he saw lying half-developed or in an environment foreign to them. That he instantly recognized where they belonged to and saw them in complete form and full of dignified potentialities—this is the unintelligible part of the business. Here his mind worked like a force of Nature which far outstrips all calculating investigation." [1]

Elsewhere Chrysander, in speaking of the *Ode for St. Cecilia's Day*, more than half of which contains elements derived from Muffat's harpsichord music, says :

"That everything has become Handelized down to its subtlest characteristics, no unbiassed judge can for a moment fail to recognize. But it is equally indubitable that Handel's music has gained much in value in all directions by the insertion of melodious matter due to others. This practice of employing as models and material existing pieces of his own or others, was in him not an affair of accident but of principle, and pervades all his writings." [2]

In our study of *Israel in Egypt* we saw decisive proofs that Handel possessed a quite astonishing power of seizing on older music, his own or that of others, raising it to a far higher level, and transfusing it with a nobler life. Where he did this, it is not too much to say, with Chrysander, that the material taken over "became his own" in the sense which I understand to be here intended, viz. that

---

[1] Chrysander : Life of Handel, vol. I, p. 176.

[2] Chrysander. Preface to edition of Muffat's *Componimenti*, p. IV.

what Handel added was of an incomparably higher order than what he took.   But this only applies to instances where he is felt to be working with strokes of genius, or, to use Chrysander's happy phrase "like a force of Nature."   In so 'inspired' a work as *Israel* there are, indeed, many such great moments, but also considerable tracts where the alterations effected do not go beyond what might be expected from a first rate teacher of composition correcting, and improving on, work by a talented pupil.   In these the "melodious matter due to others" by the insertion of which Handel's music "gained much in value" may not unfairly rank equally with the greater man's contribution or, if the alterations have been insignificant, may even claim the first place.   In the case of practically note-for-note transference of entire movements such as the two choruses by Graun and the canzona by Kerl, it appears to me impossible to claim that they have by this simple process "become Handel's own."

That, as a matter of fact, Handel gave a new lease of life to musical ideas, his own or others', which if left in their original forms would have been no more heard of, is of course indisputable.   But Dr. Chrysander, as we have just seen, while recognizing that "his music has gained much in value by the insertion of melodious matter due to others" asserts that Handel was led to his practice of working up pre-existing material by "the impulse of his artistic nature to save from perishing musical ideas which he saw lying half-developed or in an environment foreign to them."

This is an hypothesis which one would be very glad to believe true.   Dealing, however, as it does, with the *motives* of a man dead nearly a century-and-a-half ago from whom no utterance about them has been handed down to us or even asserted to have been made to any of his contemporaries, it is evidently susceptible neither of proof nor of disproof.   A probable judgment on it could only be reached by examining in what proportions Handel's rearrangements of material show development and improved environment, or appear merely to have been made for the temporary convenience of a composer who was also an *impressario* carrying on a campaign which involved the constant production of 'novelties.'   The examination would be an interminable one and all the materials required for making it have probably even yet not been collected.   That its result would bear out the sweeping assertions of Dr. Chrysander I hesitate to believe.

Quite apart from what may have been Handel's *motives*, his *action* raises a question of morals which must be considered here.   The nature of that question has been stated and discussed very clearly and suggestively by the Right Hon. A. J. Balfour, M.P., in the following passage extracted from his extremely able and interesting essay on Handel:[1]

"But, it will be said, the question of morality still remains.   It cannot be right

---

[1] Essays and Addresses, 2nd edition.   Edinburgh : David Douglas, 1893.

for a great writer to appropriate the work of a small one, and at the same time wrong for a small one to appropriate the work of a great one. Bare justice requires that a common rule should apply to both.

"I will not venture on a full discussion of the casuistical problem thus raised. An interesting chapter remains to be written on the history of "private property in thought." When this is accomplished, it will become clear, I believe, that while, at the revival of learning and before it, the unwritten code regulating such matters was so lax that it was by no means considered necessary to acknowledge even direct quotations, the monopoly has become stricter and stricter down to our own time. And it will also be found that some of the greatest and most original geniuses—Shakespeare, for instance, and Molière—have distinguished themselves by the readiness with which they have made use of other men's inventions. Among such is Handel; and with regard to him, and before finally dismissing this topic, I will only make two further observations.

"The first is, that he does not himself seem to have regarded it as a thing to be ashamed of. Among the most astonishing feats of appropriation which are laid to his charge is the wholesale transference of large fragments of a "Magnificat" by an obscure musician of the name of Erba, to the score of "Israel in Egypt." Now, one of the only two copies of this "Magnificat" known to exist is in Handel's handwriting, and is preserved among his manuscripts at Buckingham Palace. But what is the history of these manuscripts? They are by no means casual chips from his musical workshop, scraped together from holes and corners, and arranged for the first time after his death. On the contrary, Handel himself, always sedulous of his fame, set the greatest store by them. He intended leaving them to his amanuensis, the elder Smith. He quarrelled with Smith, and then proposed to leave them to the University of Oxford. He and Smith afterwards became reconciled, and he reverted to his original intentions. If, therefore, we are to believe that in employing Erba's materials he was committing what he considered, or what, in his opinion, others might consider, a breach of morality, we must suppose him to be guilty of the extraordinary folly of leaving the evidence of his misdemeanour in a convenient and carefully-preserved shape among the papers on which he relied for the honourable perpetuation of his memory. And we must further suppose that he could venture to quarrel with a man so intimately acquainted with all the secrets, and according to the hypothesis the discreditable secrets, of his method, as was Smith; and that with the fate of Buononcini before his eyes, in a country which possessed its share of learned musicians,[1] and where

---

[1] "Among the most learned of whom was Dr. Pepusch, whom Handel had ousted at Cannons, and who had compiled the "Beggars' Opera" which ruined Handel's operatic speeulations." [Note by Mr. Balfour.] Additional force is given to this argument by the fact that Pepusch was, as we saw above (p. 176), one of the Directors of the Academy of Ancient Music *personally* active in bringing about the public exposure of Buononcini.

Handel possessed more than his share of open enemies and jealous friends, he was prepared to risk reputation and livelihood at once in order to save himself a few hours' extra exertion.

"My second observation is this. If the main objection to robbery consists in the fact that the victim of the robbery is injured by it, Handel's appropriation of the music of his predecessors would seem to be innocent, if not meritorious. So far from their being injured by it in the quarter in which injury was alone possible, namely, their reputation, it is not too much to say that their whole reputation is entirely founded on it.⌐ Who would take the slighest interest in Urio if Handel had not condescended to use his "Te Deum" in "Saul" and the "Dettingen?" Who would ever have heard of Erba if Handel had not immortalised him by introducing parts of his "Magnificat" into "Israel?" The fact is that Handel has not cheated them *out of* their due meed of fame, he has cheated them *into* it. And I apprehend that if this were made a preliminary condition of all literary or artistic pilfering, the art of plagiarism would not in all probability be extensively practised or grossly abused." (pp. 152-156.)

A comparison between Shakespeare, Molière and Handel in regard to their use of sources might doubtless lead to interesting results, and the similarity between them as being all three connected with theatres, for which they had to produce under pressure, of itself invites such a comparison. Its result could not, however, supply evidence bearing on our present enquiry comparable in importance with that afforded us by the Buononcini affair as showing that in the time of Handel plagiarism in music was regarded just as it is now. The first Copyright Act (8 Anne, cap. 19), passed in 1709, under which proceedings were also taken in defence of musical property,[1] shows, too, that a stricter view of literary ownership had by that time found utterance in legislation.

Mr. Balfour argues that Handel, if conscious of having used a *Magnificat* by Erba in a way which, once detected, was likely to ruin both himself and his reputation, would never have included his own autograph copy of that work among the collection of volumes which, bequeathed to his amanuensis, the elder Smith, are now in the Library of Buckingham Palace.

The case which Mr. Balfour makes out is undoubtedly strong, but is subject, I think, to certain deductions. As Handel's autograph of the *Magnificat* bore no composer's name, it was only likely to be used against his authorship if and when independent external evidence was forthcoming to show that the work was the composition of another. *Then*, no doubt, Handel's autograph might play an important part in settling the question of priority, but equally possibly a non-Handelian authorship might be completely established *without* its aid. The risk

---

[1] Encyclopædia Britannica : article 'Copyright.'

of retaining the autograph in Handel's collection is somewhat reduced by these considerations.[1]

Mr. Balfour has limited his argument to the single case of the disputed *Magnificat*, but it is equally applicable to the survival among the Fitzwilliam autographs of many passages copied by Handel from the works of Continental composers and afterwards incorporated in his own. That he did not destroy these copies may indeed be accepted as showing that he considered himself to have committed no breach of morality towards the composers concerned. But that he considered other people likely to take the same view of these appropriations— notably of the two long ones from Graun, which go to the very verge of the Buononcini procedure—*this* I am unable to join Mr. Balfour in believing.

The point so forcibly put about the benefits which Handel conferred on the reputations of his predecessors by appropriating their music, loses some of its force if we remember that these appropriations were invariably made *without acknowledgment,* just as in Handel's Fitzwilliam extracts the name of the composer copied from is in no single instance recorded. How then can the reputation of a predecessor be said to have gained by the credit due to him for something he had written having been absorbed by Handel? No doubt, now that the fact and sources of these appropriations have become known, an historical interest is taken in composers like Urio and Habermann which is wholly due to the use made by Handel of music written by them. But this interest is restricted within the narrow circle which concerns itself with musical history, where these composers' reputations will be measured by the intrinsic value of their works, not by the fact that Handel saw fit to make use of them. To the bulk of the music-loving world the very names of Stradella, Clari, Muffat and the rest are unknown and likely to remain so.

If, however, it be asked what has been the effect of Handel's action, not on the *reputations* but on the *musical ideas*, of the composers from whose works he borrowed, the answer given must be a very different one. Even when he merely took over matter substantially unchanged, he first gave it a fresh hearing under, in most cases, greatly improved conditions of performance, and then, by leaving it embodied in his own scores, bequeathed to it further opportunities of being heard. But in the much more numerous instances where he subjected what he had borrowed to a process of reconstruction, he was able to breathe a new life into it and, by working it up into one or other of his most inspired efforts, seems to have even secured— as far as this is humanly attainable—that it should be " had in everlasting remembrance."

That the musical world is the richer for the way in which Handel used

[1] This remark is of course made on the assumption that Erba composed the *Magnificat*, which is the view here taken for granted by Mr. Balfour.

thematic materials due to his predecessors and his contemporaries can hardly be doubted. Surely, however, he could equally well have conferred that boon if he had openly acknowledged his obligations to other composers. But, as matters stand, the fact remains that he accepted, indeed practically claimed, merit for what he must have known was not his own work. That this was wrong can, it appears to me, be denied by those only who are prepared to estimate the morality of an act according to the amount of genius shown in performing it.

APPENDIX.

LIST OF WORKS BY HANDEL QUOTED FROM IN THIS VOLUME

LIST OF COMPOSERS, INSTANCES OF THE USE OF WHOSE WORKS
BY HANDEL ARE QUOTED IN THIS VOLUME

LIST OF EXAMPLES

LIST OF WORKS BY HANDEL QUOTED FROM
IN THIS VOLUME.

LIST OF COMPOSERS, INSTANCES OF THE USE OF
WHOSE WORKS BY HANDEL ARE QUOTED IN
THIS VOLUME.

	EXAMPLES
Clari	17
Graun	18—20
Habermann	10—16
Keiser	45—48
Kerl	31
Lotti	49
Muffat	1—9
Stradella	27, 28, 30, 34 [43?]
Urio	37

LIST OF EXAMPLES.

INDEX.

DATE DUE

NOV 1 9 1987			
DEC 1 0 1987			
DEC 1 2 1993			
DEC 1 6 1994			

DEMCO 38-297